GETTING TO GRIPS WITH

Punctuation and Grammar

CATHERINE HILTON

MARGARET HYDER

Letts EDUCATIONAL

First published 1992
Reprinted 1993

Editorial team
Rachel Grant, Andrew Thraves, Angela Royal

Design team
Frank Greenyer, Jonathan Barnard

British Library Cataloguing in Publication Data

Hilton, Catherine
    Punctuation and grammar. – (Getting to grips)
    I. Title II. Hyder, Margaret III. Series
    428

ISBN 1 85758 090 7

Printed and bound in Great Britain by Staples Printers St Albans Ltd

Acknowledgements

Every effort has been made to trace all copyright holders but, if any have
been inadvertently overlooked, the publishers will gladly receive
information enabling them to rectify any error or omission in subsequent
editions.

Pages 6 and 128, entry from *Chambers Concise Dictionary*; page 31, from the
Daily Telegraph Magazine, 8 December 1990; page 42, extract from 'When
You Are Old', by W B Yeats (Yeats - *Selected Poetry*, Pan Books Ltd); page
88, cartoon from *How to Survive Children* by K Whitehorn (Magna Books
Ltd); page 89, from *Some Lie and Some Die* by Ruth Rendell (Hutchinson
Books Ltd); page 90, from *Hitch Hiker's Guide to the Galaxy* by Douglas
Adams (Pan Books Ltd).

Contents

How to Use this Book 5

How to Use this Book

We hope this book will help you to improve your punctuation and grammar so that you can write more freely, effectively and confidently.

The chapters are arranged in such a way as to allow you to work through each section systematically or, if you prefer, you can dip into the chapters in any order according to your needs.

For ease of access, the book is divided into two sections: Section 1 deals with Punctuation and Section 2 with Grammar. However both sections are interrelated, as punctuation and grammar go hand in hand. For example, in Section 1 we introduce the idea of writing in sentences, consider what makes up a sentence and how to punctuate sentences. As every sentence we write is made up of grammatical elements, then punctuation, to some extent, depends upon knowing about grammatical structures.

Section 1 – Punctuation

▶ You are shown the main rules governing the use of punctuation marks.

▶ There is advice on how to use them in your writing.

Section 2 – Grammar

▶ The function of words is discussed.

▶ We consider how words group together.

▶ Many common errors are outlined, with advice on how they can be avoided.

1
Introducing Punctuation

Punctuation, the act or art of dividing sentences by points or marks.

(from *Chambers Concise Dictionary*)

Each language has its own established conventions for the use of punctuation marks and capital letters. These have been developed over the years and are based on the history of the language and habit. Like spelling, word meanings and writing style, punctuation has also slowly changed over the centuries.

If you look at books from the last century or earlier this century, you will see that the style of writing was generally more complex and elaborate. Sentences were often longer and involved the use of numerous commas and semicolons. Nowadays it is fashionable to write in a more straightforward way, often using shorter sentences, so using fewer commas and semicolons. Thus less punctuation is used.

What is punctuation?

▶ It is an established code of signs which allows people to make sense of writing.

▶ It is one of the skills of writing.

▶ It is a necessary part of any piece of writing.

The established code

Punctuation can cause a great deal of disagreement for although there are certain basic rules, there are also options and personal preferences which allow us to develop our own individual style. The main purpose of punctuation is to make the written word perfectly clear to the reader.

We write in order to convey information, thoughts, experiences, feelings, ask questions and seek advice. We want to communicate with others and we want them to understand what we have written. There is, after all, no point in writing unless others can understand what we have written.

Natural punctuation

When we speak, we automatically use punctuation by inserting pauses to allow our listener to understand our conversation. We also give our listener many other clues to help him or her understand our message. Our voices go up and down, we emphasise certain words and use different tones of voice. Gestures and facial expressions also aid our audience. We can tell from our audience's reaction if our message has been understood. If it hasn't, we have the opportunity to make amends.

Obeying the code

In writing we are unable to give our audience so many clues. Usually we do not see our audience's reaction to our writing and cannot add to or alter our message after it has been completed so we need to make certain that our message is clear and unambiguous. First we choose the words we want to say, we arrange them in the correct order and then we replace the pauses, rises, falls and tone of speech with punctuation marks so that readers can understand what we mean. As we want everyone who reads our writing to interpret it in the same way, we have to use a standard code that everyone understands. In writing we do not have a second chance to get our meaning across, so we need to follow the punctuation code.

One of the writing skills

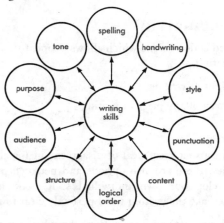

Obviously the words we choose to convey our ideas and the way we put them together are most important but correct punctuation reinforces their meaning. Punctuation is an important aspect of good writing but the content, style and interest value of our writing are the prime consideration.

What does punctuation do?

▶ It helps us to make sense of what we read.

▶ It helps others to understand our writing.

▶ It helps us when reading aloud.

▶ It separates one group of words from another.

▶ It gives the reader clues and special information.

Understanding

A passage which is correctly punctuated will separate words which go together into groups of different sizes so that their meaning is clear, thus enabling us to understand the meaning of the entire passage and the parts within it. All of us will have had experience of reading a difficult or lengthy sentence several times to unlock its meaning. When we read a difficult passage, we rely on punctuation points to help us interpret it. By pausing at the punctuation points, we concentrate on one idea at a time, allowing this to sink in before we tackle the next idea.

Reading aloud

When we read aloud, we want to be as effective as possible and allow our audience not only to appreciate our message but also to derive pleasure from it. We separate the passage into manageable units by emphasising the pauses made by the full stops, commas and semicolons. Our voices display emotion when we encounter exclamation marks or go up at the end of a sentence which poses a question. Our voices follow the rhythm of the sentence as we interpret the punctuation code.

Separators and informers

Punctuation marks can serve different purposes within a sentence.

Separators

A sentence is a group of words that go together to form a unit which makes sense. At the end of each sentence there is a full stop, question mark or exclamation mark, which separates this sentence from the next. Within a sentence commas, semicolons and colons separate one group of words from another.

Informers

Punctuation marks such as question marks, exclamation marks, quotation marks and apostrophes give the reader clues. Question marks and exclamation marks are both separators and informers.

e.g. An apostrophe can show ownership or use:

The boy's bikes ...

The boys' bikes ...

This ownership is shown very precisely by the use and position of the apostrophe.

Why does punctuation matter?

> In his last two years at school he managed to find a Saturday job which he thoroughly enjoyed he worked at a chemists shop where he served customers stocked the shelves filed prescriptions counted out tablets priced items and delivered medicines to the elderly all this gave him valuable experience with meeting people and subsequently helped him with his future career

In the passage above, the correct words have been chosen and arranged in the right order but the meaning of the words is not immediately clear without punctuation marks.

Punctuation helps us understand written material.

The passage is even more difficult to read if it is incorrectly punctuated because we, as readers, are used to following the punctuation code and if given the wrong signals, the message becomes distorted.

> In his last two years. At school he managed to find a Saturday job. Which he thoroughly enjoyed he worked. At a chemist's shop. Where he served customers stocked. The shelves filed prescriptions. Counted out tablets priced. Items and delivered, medicine to the elderly all. This gave him valuable experience with meeting. People and subsequently helped him. With his future career.

With the punctuation marks in the wrong places, the passage is nonsensical. (If you wish to see this passage punctuated correctly, it is on page 33 in Chapter 4.)

Punctuation gives precise meaning to our writing.

Look at these sentences:

<u>Sentence 1</u> Ian's father is going to arrive on Sunday.

<u>Sentence 2</u> Ian's father is going to arrive on Sunday!

<u>Sentence 3</u> Ian's father is going to arrive on Sunday?

In each case the words and the word order are the same but each one ends in a different punctuation point which alters the meaning of the sentence.

Sentence 1 is a statement of fact; sentence 2, by the use of an exclamation mark, indicates amazement or surprise, while sentence 3 is a question.

In some examinations, marks are deducted for poor punctuation and further marks may be lost if lack of punctuation, or poor punctuation, prevents your message from being conveyed accurately. Examiners frequently complain about poor or haphazard punctuation in examination scripts, whether these be in English or other subjects. In English exams the most serious fault is a failure to write in sentences. Candidates often link several sentences together without separating them with full stops and/or use commas where full stops are required. Both of these are considered to be basic errors.

How can you improve?

▸ Work through the chapters in Section 1 so that you develop an understanding of the basic uses of the punctuation points.

▸ Build your punctuation skills by using them as much as possible. Write! Write! Write!

▸ Use your common sense. You are using punctuation to make your writing clear and unambiguous so use the least amount of punctuation that will result in exact meaning.

▸ If you were speaking, you would use the correct punctuation automatically so try to reproduce this skill as you write. Think out what you want to say in your head before you commit it to paper. If you are working in a room alone, you may find it helps to think aloud. By noticing where you pause in speech, you can reflect this in your writing.

▸ Always proof-read your work. Whenever possible, read it aloud, stressing the pauses made by the full stops and commas.
Ask yourself:
    does it make sense?
    are there any points where an extra comma would make the
    sense clearer?
When checking your punctuation, concentrate on what you have written and question whether it is exact, clear and can be easily understood by others.

▸ You will soon begin to identify your weak points so always have a special check for these when you proof-read.

▸ Be an alert and observant reader. By noticing how the passages you read are punctuated, you can compare their styles to that of your own writing. Try reading a passage aloud from a well-written newspaper or magazine. Obey the punctuation marks and exaggerate the pauses to draw them to your attention. Question why certain points of punctuation have been used and try to justify their use.

▸ Watch and listen to television newsreaders, noticing the pauses which separate one group of words from another. These pauses give meaning to their words.

▸ Use this book as a reference source. If you are uncertain of a particular punctuation mark, refresh your memory by going over the relevant chapter again.

▸ Be confident in your writing. You have something you want to say, so say it clearly and punctuate it correctly so that you can impart your message effectively.

Final thoughts

As you work through Section 1, you will build up the necessary basic knowledge of punctuation which should give you confidence in handling punctuation and increase your ability to write clear, unambiguous English for both everyday use and examination purposes. Punctuation is one of the writing skills. Learn the basic rules, use your common sense and use just sufficient punctuation so that your writing can be clearly understood.

2
Sentences

APPLICATION FOR EMPLOYMENT

Personal Details

Name Ray Ryder

Address 4 Station Street

Brentford

Essex

BR2 4RQ

Tel. no. 0654 34221

Date of birth 28/8/53

Marital status married

No. of children 4

Occupation taxi driver

Name of previous employer Alpha Cars Ltd

If you were asked to describe the person whose details are given above, you would probably say something like this:

"Ray Ryder lives in Brentford. He is thirty-nine years old and is married with four children. He worked for Alpha Cars as a taxi driver."

Although the information wasn't shown in sentences, you would probably have used sentences when you described Ray Ryder as sentences make up our natural units of speech (see Chapter 1).

What is a sentence?

A sentence is a group of words which makes complete sense.

EXAMPLES:

Paul's car cost £5000.

The office will close at 1.00 pm.

There were terrible floods during December.

I think watching snooker on television is boring.

Each of these sentences expresses a complete idea.

Sentences can be statements, questions, commands or exclamations.

Statements

These express a fact or opinion.

EXAMPLES:

The briefcase burst open. (fact)

I think it is too heavy. (opinion)

Questions

These are sentences which require an answer.

EXAMPLES:

Is it too heavy?

Are you going to work today?

Commands

These issue an instruction, saying what must or must not be done. They will vary in tone depending on the situation.

EXAMPLES:

Use two eggs. (an instruction in a cookery recipe)

Do not walk on the grass. (a notice on a housing estate)

Exclamations

These show emotional outbursts expressing joy, sympathy, dismay, anger, etc.

EXAMPLES:

What a wonderful day it is!

How awful for you to fail!

The punctuation of sentences

In speech the rhythm or tone of voice usually indicates whether we are asking a question, making a statement or expressing our feelings.

Read these sentences aloud:

Sentence 1 Are you going out?

Sentence 2 The assistant gave me my change.

Sentence 3 What a lovely present you gave him!

The clues to help you read these in the appropriate manner are shown by each sentence's final punctuation mark. Sentence 1 is asking a question and ends in a question mark. The word order and the question mark combine to help you use the correct tone of voice when you read this sentence. Sentence 2 ends with a full stop and is making a statement. Your tone of voice will reflect this. Sentence 3 expresses pleasure. The exclamation mark helps you to put the right degree of warmth and enthusiasm into your voice when you read this sentence.

These final punctuation marks help the reader make sense of the words, read them correctly and gain the right interpretation from them.

A sentence ends with either a full stop, a question mark or an exclamation mark. To indicate the start of a sentence clearly, a capital letter is used for the first letter of the first word.

Punctuating sentences

** Put a full stop, question mark or exclamation mark at the end of each of these sentences.

1 Who is that person over there

2 I hope he is all right

3 What a lovely dog they have

4 Don't do that

5 Please can I come with you

6 I expect he'll be late tonight

7 Follow the advice given on the packet

8 Which restaurant shall we go to

You will find more about these punctuation points in Chapter 5.

Why write in sentences?

▶ to make meaning clear
▶ they are the hallmark of correct English

Clear meaning

> Barry,
>   Gone to keep-fit.
> Dinner in oven. Back
>   9.30 ish.
>   Pat

On reading this, Barry would probably assume that Pat has gone to keep–fit; Barry's dinner is in the oven and Pat will be back at about 9.30 pm.

But as the note isn't written in sentences, it could be interpreted in another way. It could mean that Pat and/or someone else has gone to keep–fit and that Barry is to put her/their dinners in the oven for when she/they return at about 9.30 pm.

If Barry knows Pat well and they are aware of each other's lifestyles, then the note is probably adequate, but when we wish to make our written message absolutely clear, we need to write in sentences.

Hallmark of good English

Knowledge of sentence construction and the correct punctuation of sentences are the basic requirements of most formal writing tasks. Remember: writing in sentences helps us to express our ideas clearly. Examiners in English examinations consider the ability to write in sentences an essential skill. Examiners of other subjects will also expect answers to be written in sentences if an essay-type response is required. Although the subject content of such essays is of prime importance, your ideas may not be correctly understood unless they are expressed in sentences.

Unless you have recently attended an English class, you may have only a vague idea about sentence construction. You may also be in the habit of not writing in sentences. Such a habit can be hard to break. However, after working through this chapter and Chapters 3 and 5, you should have a clearer and fuller understanding of sentence construction.

How to recognise a sentence

Read these examples.

hoped to see you

Robert writes long letters

Val and John

books are expensive

Which of these examples are sentences?

Only two of these examples make complete sense:

Robert writes long letters.

and

Books are expensive.

How do sentences make sense?

A sentence is made up of two parts: the subject and the predicate.

The subject

The subject of a sentence is who or what the sentence is about.

e.g. In the sentence

Robert writes long letters.

the subject is 'Robert', as the sentence is about him and what he does.

The subject of a sentence is usually a noun or a pronoun. (A noun is a 'naming' word. A pronoun can be used to replace a noun. See Chapters 12 and 13.)

The predicate

The predicate provides information about the subject.

'writes long letters' is the predicate of the sentence above. It tells us what Robert (the subject) does.

The predicate contains a verb. (A verb is a word or words which describe an action or a state of being. See Chapter 14.)

The example 'Val and John' is not a sentence as the words do not make complete sense, although they could form part of a sentence.

EXAMPLES:

Val and John <u>came to dinner</u>.

    subject   predicate

Val and John play <u>tennis</u>.

    subject   predicate

In these examples the words 'Val and John' have become the subject of a sentence and have had further words added (the predicate) to give information about the subject. The words now make complete sense and so form a sentence.

Similarly, in the example 'hoped to see you', we have been given a predicate but no subject. The words will only make complete sense when we are told who or what the subject is.

e.g. Vivienne <u>hoped to see you</u>.

    subject   predicate

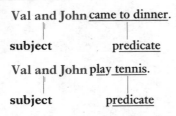

Sentences make complete sense and have a subject and a predicate. The predicate contains a verb and gives information about the subject.

** Supply a suitable subject for each of these phrases.

1 moved slowly	6 are very interesting
2 is leaving on Monday	7 wanted to help
3 was made redundant	8 have the necessary funds
4 is driving at 40 mph	9 was wandering aimlessly
5 barked angrily at the postman	10 wrote a memo to the staff

** Use each of the following as the subject of a sentence.

1 Mr and Mrs Haywood	6 rugby
2 the president	7 inflation
3 police	8 India
4 employees	9 clothes
5 Rachel	10 happiness

Identifying the subject and predicate

** Find the subject and predicate of each of these sentences.

1 Journalists were warned to stay clear of the area.
2 Fifteen thousand fans attended the concert.
3 Kurt plays squash regularly.
4 That young couple bought Norma's house.
5 The weather has been wonderful recently.
6 It must have cost a great deal.
7 Football is popular in many countries.
8 They were wrong.

Sentence checklist

If you are still uncertain about your ability to write in sentences, try applying this checklist:

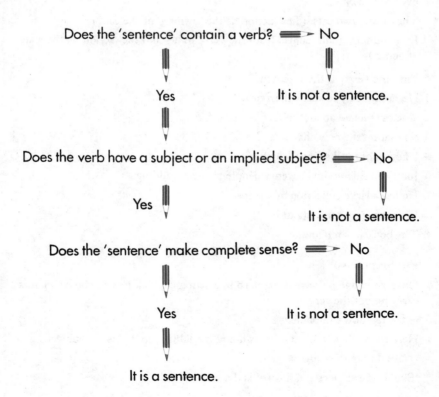

Does the 'sentence' contain a verb? ➡ No

Yes   It is not a sentence.

Does the verb have a subject or an implied subject? ➡ No

Yes   It is not a sentence.

Does the 'sentence' make complete sense? ➡ No

Yes   It is not a sentence.

It is a sentence.

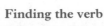

Finding the verb

A verb describes an action.

EXAMPLES:

thinks

licked

buy

kick

Some verbs are easier to identify than others. When a clear action is taking place, the verb is obvious.

EXAMPLES:

The supporters cheered their team.

He whistled happily.

However, sometimes the action is more passive and so more difficult to spot.

EXAMPLES:

They have two cats. (The 'action' is the 'owning' of the cats.)

I am hungry. ('am' comes from the verb 'to be' and the 'action' is the state of being.)

** Find the verbs in these sentences.

1 He ran quickly towards the exit.

2 The car moved about ten feet.

3 She sat on the new chair.

4 They slept until seven o'clock.

5 John and Sue invited seventy people to their wedding.

6 He has a large collection of stamps.

7 We were very sorry about it.

8 The book was too long.

Finding the subject

Once you have identified the verb in a sentence, look to see who or what is carrying out the action.

He fell down the hole.

Here the verb is 'fell' and 'he' is doing the falling, so 'he' is the subject.

She broke the camera.

'She' is the subject and 'broke' is the verb.

Sometimes more than one person or thing makes up the subject of a sentence.

Mr and Mrs Patel visited me yesterday.

'Mr and Mrs Patel' are the subject of this sentence as both carried out the action 'visiting'.

Silver and gold are both precious metals.

'Silver and gold' are the subject and 'are' is the verb in this sentence.

** Look back at the previous practice exercise and identify the subject of each sentence.

Identifying sentences

** Identify which of the following are sentences. You will notice that there are no punctuation clues to help you. Remember a sentence is a unit of sense.

1 running around the garden
2 yesterday we bought a new car
3 the unhappy girl
4 where are you going
5 look at all those people
6 the oranges have gone mouldy
7 he looked angrily at the noisy children
8 at the next election
9 solar heating can be effective
10 rushing for the train

Subject is understood

In a sentence which gives a command, the subject may not actually be shown but is implicit in the meaning of the sentence.

e.g. Follow my directions.

This is a sentence. The verb is 'follow' and the person who is to carry out the action, although not actually named, is either the person who is being spoken to or the reader of the instruction. The subject is implied.

Here are further examples of sentences where the subject is not shown but is implied.

Have a nice day.

Do not smoke in this area.

Spin garment. Do not wring.

Summary

Sentences

▶ make complete sense
▶ have a predicate which contains a verb
▶ have a subject, which is usually either a noun or a pronoun

Sentences can be

▶ statements
▶ questions
▶ commands
▶ exclamations

Sentences

▶ start with a capital letter
▶ end with a full stop, a question mark or an exclamation mark

Final thoughts

This chapter has looked at sentences in considerable detail because they are so important in writing. By now you should have a fuller understanding of sentence construction and be feeling more confident about your ability to write in sentences. Although this may appear to be a fairly simple skill, it is easy to make mistakes. When checking through your work, look carefully at your sentences and, if you are uncertain, apply the checklist. Remember that in formal writing, sentence construction is crucial to making your message clear. It is also important to have plenty of practice in writing; completing exercises is only part of the practice you need. If you are still having difficulty with writing in sentences, then take a second look at this chapter. Chapter 3 also deals with sentence construction and there will be further practice in later chapters to help you develop a greater understanding of sentences.

3
More About Sentences

In Chapter 2 you were shown that a sentence:
▶ makes complete sense
▶ has a verb with a subject

e.g. He <u>noticed</u> the abandoned car.

subject <u>verb</u>

This chapter gives you further practice in identifying sentences and looks at different types of sentence construction so helping you to:
▶ understand punctuation
▶ develop your writing style
▶ check for correct punctuation

Phrases

Do these make sense?

<u>Example 1</u> running away

<u>Example 2</u> to be the leader

<u>Example 3</u> on the stairs

They make some sense but not complete sense. These and other similar word groups are called **phrases**.

A phrase is a group of words which makes partial sense.

In <u>Example 1</u> we don't know who or what is running away. We could add a subject

Helen running away
but this still does not make complete sense.
We need to add 'is' or 'was' for the sentence to make complete sense.

Helen is running away. (a sentence)

Helen was running away. (a sentence)

<u>Examples 2 and 3</u> are also phrases; they make partial sense but are not complete

sentences. They require a subject and a verb before they form complete sentences.

EXAMPLES:

He has always wanted to be the leader.

The dog was lying on the stairs.

Using phrases

** Use each of these phrases in a sentence. Remember to start each sentence with a capital letter and end with the correct punctuation mark.

1 at twelve o'clock
2 along the road
3 thinking of you
4 very pleased with themselves
5 under the bridge
6 currently working in London
7 to put the matter right
8 to find work

Well-known phrases

You are probably more aware of phrases than you realise, as in our everyday conversation we often use or hear colourful phrases that either summarise our feelings or express our ideas in a topical way.

Sentence length

Birds sing.

This is a sentence although it consists of only two words. If you applied the sentence 'checklist' you would see that:

▶ it has a verb, 'sing'

▶ the verb has a subject, 'birds'

▶ the sentence makes complete sense

This is also a sentence:

> During his budget speech, the Chancellor of the Exchequer announced an increase in personal allowances to take effect from the start of the financial year.

Sentences can vary in length and complexity.

Types of sentences

▶ Simple sentences

▶ Double sentences

▶ Multiple sentences

▶ Complex sentences

What is a simple sentence?

The word 'simple' used in this way has nothing to do with the content of the sentence but refers to its construction. A simple sentence contains one verb and its subject.

e.g. He <u>walked</u> to work.

    subject   <u>verb</u>

Remember a simple sentence can vary in length:

EXAMPLES:

He <u>walked</u>.

subject <u>verb</u>

He <u>walked</u> five miles to work every day during the bus strike.

subject   <u>verb</u>.

These are all simple sentences.

Double sentences

Two simple sentences may be formed into one double sentence by linking them with conjunctions such as 'and', 'but', 'or'.

EXAMPLES:

He <u>likes</u> football. He <u>enjoys</u> cricket.

subject <u>verb</u>   subject <u>verb</u>

He likes football and enjoys cricket.

Susan <u>lives</u> in Southend. She <u>works</u> in London.

subject <u>verb</u>   subject <u>verb</u>

Susan lives in Southend but works in London.

Guidance

'and' is used to link closely related sentences.

e.g. The house was old **and** was beginning to fall down.

'but' is used to link closely related sentences where a contrast is made.

e.g. Tony is a vegetarian **but** he eats fish.

You can link sentences together which don't have the same subject but they must make sense when joined together.

e.g. The weather was wet. We went out for a walk.

     subject   subject

The weather was wet, but we went out for a walk.

Why use double sentences?

Read this holiday information about a Greek island:

> Have a wonderful time on Maxos. The sun always shines. It hardly ever rains. You can lie on sandy beaches. You can swim in a crystal-clear sea. Food on Maxos is cheap. Wine is even cheaper. The people are friendly. They are always willing to talk to you about their island. Enjoy the best things in life on Maxos.

Because this brief passage is made up of several short sentences and we have to pause at each full stop, it sounds disjointed. Compare this with the first passage:

> Have a wonderful time on Maxos. The sun always shines **and** it hardly ever rains. You can lie on sandy beaches **or** swim in a crystal–clear sea. Food on Maxos is cheap **but** wine is even cheaper. The people are friendly **and** are always willing to talk to you about their island. Enjoy the best things in life on Maxos.

By linking some of the sentences with 'and', 'but', 'or', the passage has lost some of its rather jerky style and sounds more fluent.

Helpful Hints

When the sentences 'You can lie on sandy beaches' and 'you can swim in a crystal–clear sea' were joined, the 'You can' of the second sentence was omitted so that the same words weren't repeated.

You can lie on sandy beaches or (you can) swim in a crystal–clear sea.

Some sentences in the passage couldn't be linked together as they were totally unrelated. For example, 'You can swim in a crystal clear sea' could not be joined with 'Food is cheap' as they wouldn't make sense together in the same sentence.

Using double sentences in your writing can help you to vary the length of your sentences and avoid a disjointed effect.

Practising double sentences

** Use 'and', 'but', 'or' to link these sentences. Omit any words which would then be repetitious.

1 The fire burnt down their house. Most of their belongings were saved.

2 I hope to visit Moscow this summer. I could wait until next year.

3 The car stalled at the traffic lights. It could not be restarted

4 Will you have some cake? Would you prefer a biscuit?

5 Hal can swim half a mile. He can tread water for ten minutes.

6 The curry was soon ready. The basmati rice took longer to cook.

7 The brake pads appear to be worn. They need to be replaced.

8 Most Saturdays Peter plays football. Sometimes he goes to watch rugby.

Multiple sentences

You have seen that two sentences can be combined to make one. Sometimes three sentences can also be linked together by using conjunctions such as 'and', 'but', 'or'.

e.g. Len was waiting for Mary to return. He kept looking down the road. Mary did not appear.

Len was waiting for Mary to return and kept looking down the road, but she did not appear.

Two or three sentences can be linked together to form one sentence by using conjunctions. Sometimes words are omitted from the original sentences to avoid unnecessary repetition.

Complex sentences

You have seen that by using double and multiple sentences you can vary the length of the sentences you write. This variety can give a more interesting style to your writing. However, if you were to use only 'and' 'or' 'but' to link sentences and only form simple, double or multiple sentences, your writing would still appear rather tedious and stilted. You may remember teachers advising you to avoid over–using 'and' in your writing. Look at the following letter and see if you agree with them.

> 24 Redwood Way,
> Harpenden,
> Glos.
> 14 January 1992
>
> Dear Giles,
>
> I hope you are well and enjoyed yourself at Christmas. We had a super time and now find it difficult to get back into the usual routine.
>
> Thank you very much for the presents you sent. The children have played with their Scalextric for hours and hours and won't even stop for food! Paul has had a few attempts at it but he is really too young and usually ends up crashing his car. Of course this results in tears and we have to calm him down and give him one of his toys to play with. I expect you're glad you aren't here and don't have to put up with all this. . . .

As you can see, 'and' has frequently been used in this letter to link sentences together. A greater variety of sentence construction could help in creating a more interesting style.

e.g. The children have played with their Scalextric for hours and hours and won't stop even for food!

Another way of writing this is

The children, who have played with their Scalextric for hours and hours, won't stop even for food!

This type of sentence construction is called 'complex'.

Look at this sentence.

When Mike phones, I shall tell him about the car.

You can see that it can be split into two parts (called clauses).

main or independent clause: **I shall tell him about the car.** (This could stand alone and makes the main statement in the sentence.)

subordinate or dependent clause: <u>When Mike phones</u>. (This depends on the main clause to make sense.)

Although it appears at the beginning of the sentence, 'when' is actually the word which links these two clauses together.

EXAMPLES:

The house <u>which is owned by Councillor Oddy</u> is for sale.

main/independent clause <u>subordinate/dependent clause</u>

link word: 'which'

Dick is always late <u>because he never wears a watch</u>.

main/independent clause <u>subordinate/dependent clause</u>

link word: 'because'

A complex sentence will always have at least one main clause; it may have more than one dependent clause.

EXAMPLES:

The horse, <u>which won its first race at Ascot</u>, was sold to Mr Forbes <u>because its previous owner had died</u>.

main/independent clause <u>subordinate/dependent clauses</u>

<u>Although I gave him no such instruction</u>, the estate agent showed several people around the house <u>before it was auctioned</u>.

main/independent clause <u>subordinate/dependent clauses</u>

There are many words that can be used to link clauses in complex sentences. **When, which, because, who, although** and **before** have been used in the examples in this chapter. Other words which can be used to link clauses include: **since, if, after, where, until, as, than, unless, while**.

** Complete these sentences.

1 The bus is late because ....

2 When the solicitor stood up, ...

3 Rita felt ill as ....

4 If you had listened to me, ...

5 The car stopped when ....

6 Since Roger passed his test, ...

7 The tyre factory closed although ....

8 John was the person who ....

Using the information given in the chart, write a short piece about domestic noise pollution. Try to vary the length and construction of your sentences.

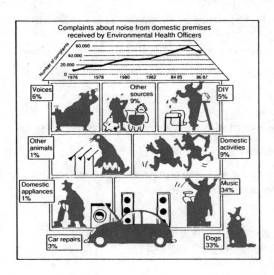

Final thoughts

Understanding the types of sentence construction should enable you to punctuate your sentences correctly, vary your style and provide you with some valuable writing tools.

However, don't assume that long, complicated sentences are necessarily better than short simple sentences. It is more effective to express your ideas clearly and simply than to attempt long rambling sentences which lose your reader.

Practice in writing and increased awareness of sentence construction will help you to develop your confidence and expertise.

Look at the sentence construction and punctuation in this extract from a newspaper. It may help to draw your attention to the ways other people punctuate their writing.

THE FAMILY

TO FEED and care for a family in Moscow is no mean task. 'Even in this situation of complete chaos, the family manages somehow to survive. I think it's because we're united, and we're optimists, all of us,' smiles Ludmilla Shcherbakova. Despite the difficulties of daily life, she and her husband Vasily have made their Moscow flat a warm, lively family home for their children Juliana, 11, and Kirill, two.

Three budgies, a guinea pig and Beauty the poodle share the family's neat two rooms, small kitchen and bathroom. Ludmilla and Vasily sleep on a sofa–bed in the living-room, while the children have the other room.

The flat was once Ludmilla's mother's, and Ludmilla has lived here for all her 34 years. 'It's already too small, but I know we won't be given a bigger one, because at 40 square metres for four people it already exceeds the living space regulations,' she says. The subsidised rent of between 25 and 30 roubles a month includes heating, electricity and gas.

(from the *Daily Telegraph Magazine*, December 1990)

CHAPTER

4
Capital Letters

It has already been mentioned in Chapter 1 that the use of capital letters in English has changed over the centuries and that their use differs from one language to another, even within European languages.

In present day English there are clear reasons for using capital letters and only in some instances does personal preference prevail.

Reasons for using capital letters

In this newspaper article, coloured print has been used for the capital letters so that your attention will be drawn to them. Read through the article and see if you can find reasons for the use of each of these capital letters.

> Mr R. Lawson, director of Branson Football Club, and his wife, Freda, were both seriously injured on Christmas Eve when their car, a Rover Vitesse, was involved in a collision on the M42 motorway, near Solihull.
>
> Peter Painter, of the Old Rectory, Burcot, who was a passenger in the back seat of the car, had a miraculous escape. After the crash he was taken to Royal Park Hospital, together with Mr and Mrs Lawson, but was discharged the following morning. "I am so lucky to be alive. Thank goodness I was wearing a seat belt. I'm sure it saved my life. I could see the accident happening and threw myself flat on the back seat."
>
> Mr Painter, who was involved in a similar accident last December, said that he was delighted to hear that the Lawsons were now out of danger and making satisfactory progress. He plans to visit them in hospital on Friday.

Capital letters are used

▶ to begin every sentence
▶ for I
▶ for proper names (proper nouns)
▶ for titles

- for days of the week, months of the year and festivals
- in letters
- to begin a new line of poetry
- for abbreviations

Beginning sentences

In Chapters 2 and 3 you saw that each sentence began with a capital letter. It is no problem remembering that a sentence begins with a capital letter, the main dilemma is understanding what a sentence is and knowing when one ends and the next begins.

When you are reading the passage below, you will notice that it is the same passage that appeared in Chapter 1. Then it was more difficult to understand, as it was first written without punctuation and then with the full stops in the wrong place. Here it is divided into sentences correctly. Pause after each full stop and follow the points from the sentence checklist in Chapter 2.

> In his last two years at school, he managed to find a Saturday job which he thoroughly enjoyed. He worked at a chemist's shop where he served customers, stocked the shelves, filed prescriptions, counted out tablets, priced items and delivered medicines to the elderly. All this gave him valuable experience with meeting people and subsequently helped his future career.

When speech is written, each new sentence requires a capital letter at the beginning.

This applies whether the dialogue is part of a passage or part of a play, as the following examples show.

> Lucy clasped and unclasped her hands and shifted from one foot to the other. She looked hot and ill at ease. Suddenly she blurted out, "It was my fault. I left the gate undone, Steven. I couldn't be more sorry about what's happened."

> HARRY   I couldn't believe my luck. It's not often you find a £20 note lying in the gutter, just waiting to be picked up. It was just outside the new sheltered housing scheme.

> SHEILA   Did you take it to the police or hand it to the care taker at the flats?

> HARRY   Neither, love. I pocketed it. Whoever dropped this

> could obviously afford to lose it. Think what it will buy us at the local.
>
> SHEILA   I'm not helping you spend it. Please, Harry, hand it in.

At times our speech consists of one word answers, partly finished sentences or phrases. **Whenever dialogue is written, the first word of each utterance needs a capital letter** whether or not it is a sentence.

STUART   Any food?

JASON   Just a sandwich.

STUART   A drink?

JASON   Coke.

PAUL   Nobody's asked ...

STUART   Sorry!

Using the guidelines

** In this short dialogue, put in the necessary end of sentence punctuation marks and a capital letter at the beginning of every sentence.

JOHN   well, officer, there were two blokes

CLIFF   no, there were three you forgot the driver in the light blue jumper who drove the green Landrover

DAVE   can I get a word in the Landrover was dark blue and his jumper was turquoise

POLICEMAN   now, now, let's have some agreement just how many men were there if we can decide on that and the colour of the Landrover, it would be most helpful do any of you recall the registration number

I

A capital letter is always used for the personal pronoun 'I', regardless of where the word occurs in a sentence.

There are no exceptions to this rule.

EXAMPLES:

I hate eating up the cold turkey after Christmas.

In September, I will be going to Scotland for two weeks.

'I' stands instead of your name. You would use a capital letter for your name. When 'I' is linked to another word to make a shortened form, it still needs a capital letter.

EXAMPLES:

I'm (I am)

I'll (I will/shall)

I'd (I would/should)

I've (I have)

You should only use this shortened form in informal writing such as letters to friends and family, or when you have to quote conversation word for word.
e.g. Riz whispered in his ear, "I'm the one they're looking for."

Proper names (proper nouns)

Place names

When you address envelopes or write an address, use capital letters for

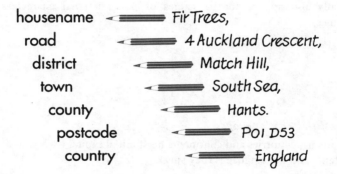

housename	◄	Fir Trees,
road	◄	4 Auckland Crescent,
district	◄	Match Hill,
town	◄	South Sea,
county	◄	Hants.
postcode	◄	PO1 D53
country	◄	England

Other place names such as names of hamlets, villages, continents, oceans, rivers, lakes, deserts and mountains also need a capital letter at the beginning.

EXAMPLES:

River Arun

Pacific Ocean

Gobi Desert

Here both words need a capital at the beginning as, each time, a particular river, ocean or desert is being named.

However, note the following examples:

I enjoy a picnic by a river.

Tim's radio broke down when he was in the middle of an ocean.

It can be bitterly cold in a desert at night.

Here, capitals aren't needed at the beginning of 'river', 'ocean' or 'desert' as these are general terms and do not refer to a specifically named river, ocean or desert.

Our names

Whenever you write your own first name or surname, use a capital letter at the beginning. This applies to everyone and so **all forenames and surnames begin with a capital letter.**

EXAMPLES:

Abdul Khan

John Major

Wendy James

This rule also applies to the names of pets, fictional characters, and nicknames.

EXAMPLES:

Rover

Garfield

Curly

Nationalities and languages

Just as towns, countries and continents need initial capital letters, so do their inhabitants and the languages they speak.

Europe	Pakistan	Italy
a European Europeans	a Pakistani Pakistanis	an Italian Italians

As you can see from the charts opposite, capital letters are also used to begin important names of:

buildings	organisations
ships	firms
brand names	words connected with religions
makes of cars/aeroplanes	political parties and theories

Other names

English Heritage
United Nations
Aston Villa Football Club
Boys' Brigade
Greenpeace
North Atlantic Treaty
Organisation

Dover Castle
University of Southampton
Foreign Office
Durham Cathedral
Taj Mahal
Rose and Crown

4

Buddhism
Hinduism
God
Allah
Bible
Koran

Lucas
American Express
Spitfire
Fiat Tempra
H.M.S. Kingfisher
S.S. Mauritania

Anadin
Frosties
Bovril
Labour Party
Communism
Democrats

Helpful Hints

When organisations are abbreviated to their initial letters, the capital letters
are retained.

e.g. NATO

  UN

Adjectives from proper names (proper nouns)

The adjectives that derive from proper nouns also require capital letters.

EXAMPLES:

noun	adjective
Dickens (name of author)	a **Dickensian** character
Elizabeth (name of queen)	an **Elizabethan** manor house
Brazil (name of country)	a **Brazilian** singer
Glasgow (name of town)	a **Glaswegian** comedian

Helpful Hints

For common objects in everyday use, capital letters are used.

EXAMPLES:

Brussels sprouts	Austrian blinds
French windows	Danish pastries
Bath buns	German measles

Capital letter practice

All the capital letters in these sentences have been omitted.

** Put in the necessary capital letters, paying special attention to the adjectives derived from proper nouns.

1 nila had always wanted a victorian brooch.

2 he has a swiss passport.

3 in this country asian culture is widely respected.

4 holland has a great variety of excellent indonesian restaurants.

5 richard is very proud of his mancunian accent.

6 the russian army is used to harsh climatic conditions.

Titles

People

Each of us has a title which must begin with a capital letter.

EXAMPLES:

Mr Plym	Mrs Jackson	Miss Simpson
Ms Rowlands	Superintendent Parker	Lord Balfour
Aunt Sue	Uncle Raymond	Doctor Greaves

Practice

** Work through this guest list and insert the capital letters.

4

GALA DINNER IN AID OF MEDICAL RESEARCH

Guest List

president bush

queen juliana

prince harry

princess caroline

king hussein

air marshal spencer

the duke of westminster

lord longford

captain walker

reverend jackson

professor hoyle

doctor owen

Helpful Hints

Titles and titles of relations begin with a capital letter when they are used with a person's name

e.g. Each Easter **Uncle Adrian** comes to stay.

or when they are used to replace an actual name.

e.g. "Come on, **Grandad**!"

But titles require small letters when they are used in other ways.

EXAMPLES:

All their mothers and fathers were invited.

Three of my aunts and two of my uncles live in Tasmania.

The education secretaries of all three countries were invited.

When titles are abbreviated, the capital letters are retained.

EXAMPLES:

The Rev. Fletcher will give tonight's sermon.

He is the M.P. for Kemp Town, Brighton.

Capt. Holdaway is now on leave.

Other titles

books   plays   poems   films   songs   television and radio programmes   newspapers and magazines   special events

In titles such as these the first word, and all the important words within the title, are written in capital letters; less important words are given lower case letters.

EXAMPLES:

The Fourth Protocol

Educating Rita

Daffodils

The Slipper and the Rose

I'm Dreaming of a White Christmas

Top of the Pops

The World at One

Daily Mirror

Classic Car

State Opening of Parliament

Days, months, dates and festivals

EXAMPLES:

Saturday, January 6th

Friday, 3rd December

Sarah will visit him one Monday in July.

All days of the week and months of the year begin with capital letters.

Special days also need capitals.

EXAMPLES:

Bank Holiday Monday

Boxing Day

New Year's Eve

Mothering Sunday

Easter

Ramadan

But the seasons of the year can be written with small letters.

e.g. winter

Letters

In letters, the greeting 'Dear' begins with a capital letter, as do 'Sir' and 'Madam' when they form the greetings 'Dear Sir' and 'Dear Madam'. The first word after the greeting also has a capital letter.

e.g. Dear Paula,

Thank you very much for a most ....

The first letter of the closing phrase should also be in capitals.

EXAMPLES:

Yours faithfully

Yours sincerely

With love

Lines of poetry

In poetry (with a few modern exceptions) each new line begins with a capital letter.

e.g.   When you are old and grey and full of sleep,
        And nodding by the fire, take down this book,
        And slowly read, and dream of the soft look
        Your eyes had once, and of their shadows deep;

(from 'When You Are Old' by WB Yeats)

4

Final thoughts

Problems can occur with certain words that appear in one instance with a capital letter and in another without. Remember the guideline – use a capital letter for the specific and a small letter when referring to the general.

EXAMPLES:

The Board meets on the first Friday of each month.

Every company has a board of directors.

Rudwick High School has an excellent exam record.

All schools in the area are closed because of the bad weather.

Organisations often have their own ideas for using capital letters. Certain job classifications can be written with an initial capital letter.

e.g. The Engineers, Planners and Architects will attend the meeting.

Follow the organisation's ruling. It doesn't matter as long as you are consistent throughout a piece of writing.

If you can master writing in sentences and using capital letters for the right reasons, you should feel confident about punctuation. The rest will soon fall into place.

Putting capital letters to the test

** Put in the necessary capital letters in these phrases.

a swiss national	london's stock exchange
the national curriculum	the indian cricket team
british medical association	the great barrier reef
the education secretary	arctic ocean
portuguese television	shrove tuesday
toyota cars	president gorbachev
korean manufacturers	british airways

Remember, capital letters are used for the particular, but not the general.

** Tick the sentences in which all the capitals have been correctly used and then correct all the other sentences.

1 He was a Captain in the army.

2 The empire state building is a tourist attraction.

3 He wanted to train to be a Doctor.

4 Clive is a Government official in Swansea.

5 Every Headmaster should receive some training in financial matters.

6 I always choose a country with Mountains for my holiday.

7 Phil Bartlett has now become bishop Bartlett.

8 Emma's special subject was the Romans.

9 My favourite book is 'the wind in the willows'.

10 Last year the whole family went to see the london marathon.

** Write an interesting sentence for each group of words below. You can use the words in any order. All the capital letters have been omitted.

chief inspector crump, new zealander, britain

i, hull, humberside, east

jill francis, mr oakham, aunt hilda, new year's day

americans, french lessons, spanish

customary, yours faithfully, dear sir

summer, tennis, wimbledon, popular

5

Punctuation in Practice

This chapter looks more closely at the punctuation marks introduced in Chapter 2:

▶ full stops
▶ question marks
▶ exclamation marks

Full stops

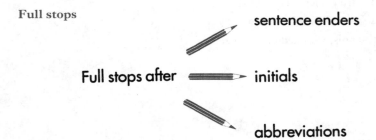

Full stops after

- sentence enders
- initials
- abbreviations

Sentence enders

A full stop is used at the end of every statement sentence and at the end of some command sentences (others end in exclamation marks).

Statement sentences

As you saw in Chapter 2, a statement sentence expresses a fact or an opinion.

EXAMPLES:

The diary was closed. (fact)

Sheila is a very pleasant person. (opinion)

Such sentences make up the majority of our speech and writing.

Sentence practice

** Divide the following passage into sentences. Start every sentence with a capital letter and end each with a full stop.

I went to see the film 'Heart Condition' last week it stars Bob Hoskins who plays a racially intolerant New York policeman after having a near fatal heart attack, he is given a heart transplant he discovers that his new heart belonged to a black lawyer who returns to haunt him it was a gripping film and one I would recommend

Command sentences

These are probably used more often in speech than in writing, as we are more likely to give a command when we are talking to someone than when we write. However, you may encounter command sentences in instruction manuals.

EXAMPLES:

Apply paste evenly.

Lever tyre away from rim.

or when direct speech (the actual words spoken) is shown.

EXAMPLES:

"Go and stand over there."

"Help me untie him."

As both of these examples end in full stops, we would assume they were expressed in an advisory rather than an emotional way. If a writer wishes to convey a strongly expressed command, an exclamation mark replaces the full stop.

e.g. "Help me untie him!" (The exclamation mark conveys urgency or panic.)

As the examples show, the tone of a command sentence can vary from the advisory to the emphatic. The full stop or exclamation mark gives the reader a clue as to the strength of emotion the writer wishes to convey.

Initials

C.A.B. – Citizens' Advice Bureau

I.T.N. – Independent Television News

D.o.E – Department of the Environment

R.S.P.C.A. – Royal Society for the Prevention of Cruelty to Animals

P.T.O. – Please turn over

R.S.V.P. – Respondez s'il vous plait (please reply)

a.m. – ante meridian

A.D. – Anno Domini (the year of our Lord)

D.I.Y. – do-it-yourself

N. Mansell – Nigel Mansell

P.D. James – Phyllis Dorothy James

It is usual to have a full stop after each initial letter of

- a company's name
- an organisation's name
- a person's name
- an accepted abbreviation

▶ While it is still common practice to use a full stop after the initial letters of a person's name, it is sometimes omitted in the other instances.

▶ Newspapers, magazines and businesses often have their own ideas in such matters and set a 'house' style.
e.g. British Telecom was at one time abbreviated to **B.T.** but is now often shown as **BT**.

As you will see both forms used, you can make your own decision about whether or not to use full stops in such instances. You can't be wrong.

▶ Usually only the important words in an organisation's name are used in the initials. Words like 'of ' and 'the' are ignored.

Abbreviations

These are commonly used in advertisements, telephone directories, dictionaries, addresses and on other occasions when we wish to express information in a limited space.

EXAMPLES:

For sale: 4 bdrm det. hse nr shops & station, lge gdn, dble grge, c. h., fully fitted kit., 2 bthrms, dng rm, lnge £99,500

Peugeot 305 – E reg. 40,000 miles, ex. cond., 1300 c.c. 6 mths MOT, £2,500 o.n.o.

In some newspaper advertisements when you are paying for each letter, brevity is important.

Look at these abbreviations. Can you see why a full stop has been used on some occasions and not others?

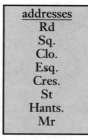

addresses
Rd
Sq.
Clo.
Esq.
Cres.
St
Hants.
Mr

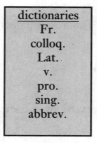

dictionaries
Fr.
colloq.
Lat.
v.
pro.
sing.
abbrev.

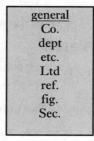

general
Co.
dept
etc.
Ltd
ref.
fig.
Sec.

5

A full stop is generally placed after the last letter of the abbreviation if that letter is different from the last letter of the actual word.

EXAMPLES:

Square becomes Sq. (The full stop is included because the last letter of 'square' is 'e'.)

Road becomes Rd (No full stop is used as 'Road' ends in 'd'.)

Dictionaries usually have a section which lists common abbreviations. If you are uncertain of the meaning of any of the examples given above, check them in your dictionary.

Metric abbreviations

No full stops are needed after these.

EXAMPLES:

1 (litre/s)   mm (millimetre/s)

g (gram/s)   cm (centimetre/s)

kg (kilogram/s)   km (kilometre/s)

Guidance

You may have noticed that the trend towards omitting full stops after initials also applies to abbreviations. Frequently in books, letters and newspapers no full stops are used after abbreviations. Once again you may follow your own preference.

If your writing has to be understood by other people, take care to use recognisable abbreviations. Often the vowels in the word are omitted in the abbreviation; the word is still recognisable from the remaining consonants.

EXAMPLES:

shwr   (shower)

bthrm   (bathroom)

For other words the accepted abbreviation is the first few letters.

EXAMPLES:

sync.   (syncromesh)

Sec.   (Secretary)

You should avoid using abbreviations in formal writing.

** Write a brief newspaper advertisement offering your house or car for sale. Use abbreviations where suitable.

Question marks

Read this extract and note where question marks have been used.

> The house was peaceful. Andrew was slumped in his favourite chair, idly turning over the pages of a magazine. He wondered where everyone had disappeared to.
>
> "Dad, do you know what Digger did while we were out?" The peace was shattered by the sound of doors slamming, a dog barking and children's voices.
>
> "Dad, where are you? Did you hear me? Digger's been naughty again."
>
> Andrew stirred in his seat. "What's the matter?" he grumbled.

Question marks are used at the end of sentences where an answer is expected. (See also rhetorical questions, page 50.)

e.g. "Dad, do you know what Digger did while we were out?"

Helpful Hints

▸ No full stop or comma is needed after a question mark.

▸ In dialogue the question mark is placed inside the speech marks (see Chapter 9).

▸ A question mark is only needed when a direct question, requiring an answer, is used.
  e.g. "Where has everyone disappeared to?" he wondered. (direct question – question mark used)

but

He wondered where everyone had disappeared to. (statement reporting on his thoughts – no question mark required)

Guidance

Avoid asking direct questions in formal letters, reports or essays. Try to replace the question with a statement which still shows the dilemma. For example,

> Will you send me the details please?

could be replaced by

> I would be grateful if you could send me the details.

Again, the sentence

> What could Nelson do?

could be rephrased as

> Nelson had to decide what to do.

Recognising questions

** Complete each of these sentences with either a full stop or a question mark.

1 How is Beth after her accident

2 Sid wanted to know if he could buy some books

3 What is the time

4 I wonder how much they charge

5 Arif asked me to tell him about our holiday

6 Where are Mr and Mrs Fisher

7 Elaine asked why they were so late

8 Alan wanted to know why he had been left out of the team

Types of questions

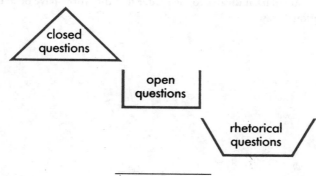

Closed questions

These need only be answered by 'yes' or 'no'.

EXAMPLES:

Have you any bananas?

Does Isabelle eat meat?

Will Dei come with us?

Open questions

These cannot be answered by 'yes' or 'no'. Such questions start with one of the question words, **what, when, where, why, how, who, which.**

EXAMPLES:

What is the date?

Where did I put it?

When will you be ready?

Why is Derek late?

How much is it?

Who was that?

Which one do you prefer?

Rhetorical questions

While these are worded in the form of a question, the questioner does not expect or wish for an answer. They may be used when a speaker, who is addressing a large group of people, poses a question.

e.g. How can we improve our service?

He does not expect the audience to suggest an answer. The question is posed for effect and he will go on to answer it himself.

Exclamation marks

An exclamation mark indicates to the reader that the words have been uttered in an emotional way.

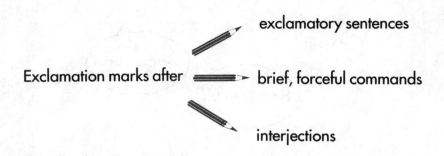

exclamatory sentences

Exclamation marks after ➡ brief, forceful commands

interjections

Exclamatory sentences

As you were shown in Chapter 2, an exclamation mark is required at the end of an exclamatory sentence. These sentences convey feelings of anger, joy, sadness, etc.

EXAMPLES:

What a terrible disaster it was!
How brave of him to volunteer!

It is possible to confuse exclamatory sentences with questions when they begin with **what** or **how**.

EXAMPLES:

What do you want? (question)

What a beautiful baby he is! (exclamation)

How lovely for you to win! (exclamation)

How do you like your tea? (question)

If you find it difficult to decide whether a question mark is required, think carefully about the meaning of the sentence. Is a question being posed? Does the sentence require an answer? If you can answer 'yes' to these questions, then you need a question mark.

Brief commands

You have already seen that on some occasions a writer will use an exclamation mark to show that a brief command has been given in a particularly forceful manner. Here are a few more examples of when an exclamation mark may be appropriate.

Be quiet!

Sit down! I have heard enough.

Don't touch that!

Interjections are words which express an emotion. They are more often used in speech than in writing but you may see or use them in written dialogue.

EXAMPLES:

"Ah! I understand now," he said triumphantly.

"Ouch! That hurt," the small boy cried.

An interjection may be followed by a comma with the exclamation mark appearing at the end of the sentence:

EXAMPLES:

"Ah, I understand now!"

"Ouch, that hurt!"

Helpful Hints

▶ The exclamation mark acts as a full stop and the next word has to start with a capital letter.

▶ Avoid using too many exclamation marks in your writing. They are rarely appropriate in formal writing situations and can easily be over-used in informal letters.

▶ To be effective, an exclamation mark should only be used when it is absolutely necessary otherwise your reader may learn not to attach any significance to it.

Final thoughts

You have now been shown and have used the main forms of punctuation: those marks which end sentences. You have also been given guidelines on using capital letters and writing in sentences. Together these form the basis of correct punctuation. If you have understood all you have been shown so far and are able to apply it correctly in your writing, you are well on your way to mastering punctuation.

6
Introducing Commas

People often complain that commas cause them problems as they are not certain when to put them in or when to leave them out. The dilemma is understandable as in certain situations where one person would include a comma, another would argue it wasn't necessary. It can be a matter of personal taste. Having said this, there are certain circumstances where commas are always needed and no disagreement should arise. If you understand the ground rules and can apply them, then commas shouldn't trouble you.

What is a comma?

A comma is used within a sentence to separate one group of words from another so that the meaning of the sentence is clear.

There is a tendency nowadays to use the minimum of punctuation so you should always have a good reason for using any punctuation mark. A comma should not interrupt the flow of the sentence and is only needed so that the reader can make sense of the written word. Although the comma is the shortest of the punctuation pauses, its inclusion and position can make all the difference to the meaning of a sentence.

A comma accords with a brief pause in speech so read each of the following sentences aloud, pausing at the commas.

Sentence 1 "Becky, our secretary has left us."

Sentence 2 "Becky, our secretary, has left us."

In sentence 1 , by pausing after 'Becky' the reader understands that Becky is being told that the secretary has left.

In sentence 2 , by pausing twice, the reader realises that Becky is the secretary who has left.

Although the words in the two sentences are the same, the sense of each is totally different. Commas are responsible for this.

Sometimes the words we read can be nonsensical when a comma is left out.

e.g. "As soon as you see him hide."

This is incomplete and doesn't make sense.

"As soon as you see him, hide."

Now it makes sense.

A comma marks a brief pause, but it can make a big difference.

The comma confusion

It is common to find a comma being used instead of a full stop. This is a basic punctuation error and it is very important to avoid it. Always write in sentences, separating each complete statement from the next by using a full stop.

e.g. I finished breakfast. I cleared away.

These are two independent, unlinked statements and need to be separated from one another with a full stop.

A comma can never do the work of a full stop.

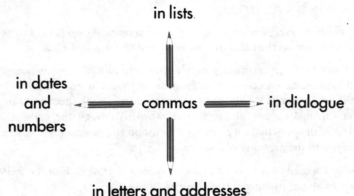

Commas in lists

Commas are used to link lists of:

▸ items
▸ groups of words
▸ adjectives
▸ actions
▸ adverbs

A list of items

EXAMPLES:

I need a stapler, a hole punch, a filing cabinet and a waste paper basket.

I am uncertain about most meat and eat only pork chops, steak or chicken.

In both examples the list part of the sentence is in coloured type. Each item in the list is separated from the next item by a comma.

There is no comma before the last item in the list as it is joined to the previous item by a conjunction.

i.e.   ... and a waste paper basket.
        ... or chicken.

Commas in a list help the reader, at a glance, to sort one item from another and make sense of a list.

6

e.g. At school she studied English history general studies combined science French geography German biology Italian cookery and mathematics.

Without commas this sentence looks rather daunting and we are uncertain about the subjects studied. Is each word in the list a separate subject or do some words belong together? Different people may have different ideas!

EXAMPLES:

English history   French geography

German biology   Italian cookery

Helpful Hints

In a list the final two items are joined by a conjunction. It is usual to omit the comma before the conjunction, but it is perfectly acceptable to use a comma if you prefer.

In some circumstances a comma before the conjunction can help the reader.

e.g. On our sponsored pub crawl we visited the Rose and Crown, Horse and Jockey, Dog and Pheasant, and the Slug and Lettuce.

Visually the comma helps to separate one pub from another.

On our sponsored pub crawl we visited the Rose and Crown, Horse and Jockey, Dog and Pheasant and the Slug and Lettuce.

Omitting the last comma causes ambiguity; the 'Slug' could be a separate pub from the 'Lettuce'.

** Write a sentence containing a list for each of these groups of words.

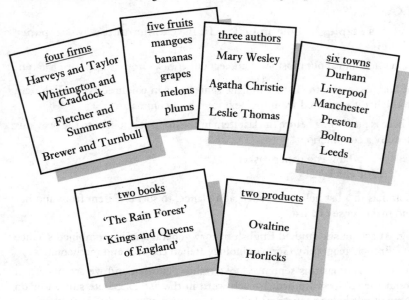

A list of groups

The items in a list do not have to be single words or pairs of words; they can also be groups of words.

EXAMPLES:

The sixth former wore jeans, a white shirt with a crumpled collar, a brightly patterned tie and trainers.

There were heathers in the bed nearest the patio, ivy, geraniums and begonias in the tubs, and clumps of fuschias bordering the lawn.

A list of adjectives

When several adjectives (describing words) are used in a sentence, they can be separated by commas.

Sentence 1 Our new accountant is friendly, amusing and talkative.

Sentence 2 His thin, pale, handsome face was just visible.

In sentence 1 the three adjectives are separated from the noun they describe. In sentence 2 the three adjectives occur before the noun they describe. No comma is needed between the final adjective and the noun it describes.

Helpful Hints

It is not always necessary to divide adjectives from one another with commas. If the adjectives describe one another, commas can be omitted.

e.g. He was wearing a **dark blue** suit and a **pale pink** shirt.

If the adjectives go together fluently, no comma is necessary.

e.g. I am trying to sell my **old blue** Cortina.

When commas are used for a list of adjectives, they have the effect of drawing attention to each individual adjective.

e.g. The plot in her new book was **tedious, complicated** and **confusing**.

When you make your decision about using commas in a list of adjectives, decide what effect you want to create.

A list of actions

e.g. The audience **booed, hissed and stamped their feet**.

The three actions are

> booed
>
> hissed
>
> stamped their feet

e.g. Each evening he **reads the paper, watches the news, does the *Daily Telegraph* crossword** and **listens to records**.

The actions in a list can be single words such as 'booed' and 'hissed', or groups of words such as 'listens to records'.

A list of adverbs

Adverbs can tell us more about verbs. When several adverbs are used to give us additional information about a particular verb, these adverbs are divided from one another by commas.

e.g. She ate her food **speedily, noisily** and **greedily**.

'speedily', 'noisily' and 'greedily' all expand upon the verb 'ate'.

Test your comma skills

** Using all the information about commas for lists, place the commas in the correct places in these sentences.

1 Family friends colleagues and business acquaintances were all invited to his fortieth birthday party.

2 She placed the cheque in the envelope sealed the envelope addressed it with care and checked it thoroughly before placing it next to the telephone.

3 The young child reached out for the soft floppy pink rabbit.

4 The group spent an enjoyable day visiting the Planetarium feeding the ducks in St James's Park watching the Changing of the Guard and shopping in Oxford Street.

5 Sieve the flour cut up the fat into small cubes and weigh out the fruit.

6 Andrew requested pleaded demanded and threatened but his brother would not let him borrow the car.

7 He wrote slowly deliberately and thoughtfully.

8 Her writing was large untidy and illegible.

Commas in dialogue

Commas are used in dialogue

▶ to separate dialogue from the rest of the sentence

▶ to address people

▶ when 'yes' or 'no' form part of an answer

▶ in interjections, some questions and asides

▶ to introduce quotations

To separate dialogue

When you write the exact words that a character uses, enclose them in speech marks.

EXAMPLES:

Jacqui shouted, "I can't help being late."

"I hope I'll understand the instructions," replied Jenny.

"Don't give it to me now," Michele said, "or I'll lose it."

The actual words spoken are separated from the rest of the sentence by a comma.

To address people

EXAMPLES:

"I know, Juliet, that you want to go to Paris."

"Juliet, I know that you want to go to Paris."

"I know that you want to go to Paris, Juliet."

When you address someone, you should separate his/her name from the rest of the sentence by one or more commas.

When speaking, we pause slightly before and after the name of the person we are addressing and we usually drop our voices when saying the name. This pause and change of tone is indicated in writing by commas. By naming the person we interrupt the flow of the sentence. The comma marks this interruption.

e.g. "Of course, you idiot, you've dropped it!"

Guidance

If you are talking *about* a person, you do not need a comma.

e.g. I know Russell is interested in astronomy.

Russell is not being spoken to. He is being talked about and no comma is needed.

'yes' or 'no' as part of an answer

EXAMPLES:

"Yes, I'd love to join in."

"No, I hate sweet things."

Again the flow of the sentence is interrupted by the inclusion of the answer 'yes' or 'no'. A comma is used to make this slight pause.

Helpful Hints

There is **no** reason for you to be afraid.

In this sentence 'no' is not an answer to a question. It is used as an adjective, describing the word 'reason', so it does not need a comma after it.

Use a comma after 'yes' and 'no' when they are used in answer to a question.

For interjections, some questions, asides

"Oh, how terrible for you!"

"Well, fancy that!"

Both of these sentences begin with an aside. The aside has a comma to separate it from the rest of the sentence. If you say each aloud, you will notice the pause.

Such asides are frequently used in conversation.

EXAMPLES:

"Naturally, I understand."

"Of course, I'll go."

In conversations we often add a question clause.

EXAMPLES:

"Nice day, isn't it?"

"Surely you'll come, won't you?"

A comma is used to separate the questioning words.

There is more about writing dialogue in Chapter 9.

For quotations

When we quote words from another person or source, a comma is used before the words are introduced. This not only takes place in dialogue but also within prose passages.

EXAMPLES:

His boss did not often listen to advice saying, "When I stop talking, I stop listening."

One soldier describes his superior as being, "One sandwich short of a picnic."

He had written, "It is better to die penniless and fulfilled than rich and unfulfilled."

Commas in addresses and letters

> 4 Lion Gardens,
> Withdean,
> Witney,
> Oxon.

It is still common practice to place a comma after each line of an address, except the last which needs a full stop. However, an increasingly popular style is to block and leave out all punctuation when writing an address, particularly if the letter or envelope is typed.

> 4 Lion Gardens
> Withdean
> Witney
> Oxon

It doesn't matter which model you choose so long as you are consistent.

If you write an address along one line, you need commas to separate the elements.

If you want to write to Jim, his address is 4 March Street, Campbell End, Lewes, Sussex.

In letters a comma is needed immediately after the name of the person you are addressing

Dear Sir,

Dear Emily,

Dear Mrs. Williams,

and after the last word of the final greeting.

Yours faithfully,

With love,

Yours sincerely,

Commas in dates and numbers

You will often see commas in dates.

EXAMPLES:

January 22nd, 1991

22nd January, 1991

August, 1975

Whilst these are perfectly acceptable, they can also be written without commas. The choice is yours.

EXAMPLES:

January 22nd 1991

22nd January 1991

August 1975

It is advisable to include a comma if one number occurs immediately after another and you feel the reader may become confused.

EXAMPLES:

Between 1950 and 1976, 970 people took part in a survey about numeracy.

On March 14, 33 civilians were killed in an air raid.

In numbers it is helpful if a comma is placed after each group of three figures. The number is easier to read.

EXAMPLES:

4,000,000

325,000

1,206

Final thoughts

In this chapter you have considered the use of commas for

    lists

      dialogues and quotations

      letters and addresses

      numbers and dates

The reasons for using them are straightforward and with practice they should not present you with any problems. In the next chapter we will look at how commas are used in more complex sentences.

▶ Be observant and notice the way other writers use punctuation as this will help to reinforce the points you have studied in this chapter.

▶ Collect several formal letters and envelopes. Look carefully at the way the addresses and dates are punctuated.

▶ Select a passage from a newspaper or magazine and see if you can find examples of commas used in lists.

▶ Find a passage of dialogue in a novel and notice the way commas are used.

7
More About Commas

Understanding sentences

In this chapter we will be looking at sentences very closely in order to find out when and where commas are needed. In Chapters 2 and 3 you saw that sentences can vary in length and complexity. It may now be helpful to recall certain points from those chapters.

A double sentence occurs when two shorter sentences are joined together by the use of a conjunction to form one longer sentence.

e.g. Simon dug over the soil. Simon planted the pansies.

Simon dug over the soil and planted the pansies.

conjunction

A main clause or independent clause is the main part of a sentence. It makes its own statement and can stand alone.

e.g. After telephoning the police,we felt more at ease.

main clause

A subordinate clause or dependent clause is the part of the sentence which gives extra information about the main clause. It cannot stand alone as it does not make complete sense by itself.

e.g. If he can have a day's leave, he will go to the computer exhibition.

subordinate clause

More uses for commas

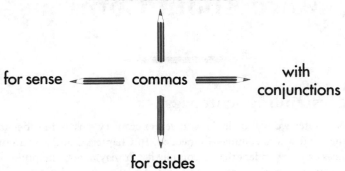

in subordinate clauses

for sense ◄ ═══ commas ═══ ► with conjunctions

for asides

Commas in subordinate clauses

Mary boarded the train.
This is a **simple sentence**.

Mary pushed through the crowd and boarded the train.
This is a **double sentence** – 'and' connects the two parts of the sentence.

No commas are needed in either of these straightforward sentences. A comma would interrupt the flow.

EXAMPLES:

Sentence 1 After pushing through the crowd, Mary boarded the train.

Sentence 2 Mary, having pushed her way through the crowd, boarded the train.

Sentence 3 When Mary had pushed her way through the crowd, she boarded the train.

In each of these sentences a commas is needed to separate one part of the sentence from another. The comma separates the parts into units of sense. If you read each sentence aloud, you will notice that it is natural to pause where the comma is placed. In speech such a pause helps your audience make sense of your message.

Commas help your reader to make sense of your writing.

In sentence 1 , 'Mary boarded the train' is the main clause. 'After pushing through the crowd' is the subordinate clause. The subordinate clause is dependent on the main clause. A comma is frequently used between the main clause and its dependent or subordinate clause, especially if the subordinate clause begins the sentence as in sentence 1 and sentence 3.

In <u>sentence 3</u>, 'she boarded the train' is the main clause. 'When Mary had pushed her way through the crowd' is the subordinate clause. If the subordinate clause at the beginning of the sentence is very long, then it is particularly helpful to put a comma after it. This helps the reader to digest one piece of information before going on to the next.

e.g. **After attending a long tutorial session to discuss his plans for the future**, he decided to join the Royal Navy.

Being able to identify the main clause in a sentence is useful because it allows you to check that you have used commas in the correct way.

Comma practice

** Put in all the necessary commas in this passage.

> Having spent the past week revising he was confident about the examination. When the paper was placed on his desk he felt excited and eager to begin.
>
> As he turned over the page and noticed the first question his heart began to pound. Despite all his revising he would not be able to attempt question one. Resting his head in his hands he tried to concentrate on the exact wording of the question hoping he had misread it at his first attempt.

Commas with conjunctions

e.g. I go dancing each Tuesday and I always enjoy it.

The conjunction 'and' joins the two parts of the sentence together. No comma is needed.

e.g. I go to English classes each week, but I do not enjoy them.

Here the conjunction 'but' joins the two parts of the sentence together. A comma has been included, but it could be omitted.

Helpful Hints

▶ A comma is usually unnecessary when 'and'/'or' are used to join two parts of a sentence together.

▶ With other conjunctions commas can also be left out, but it often helps the reader if you include them.

▶ A comma is especially helpful if you want to create a contrast or emphasise a certain point.

EXAMPLES:

I will write the essay again, although I don't think I will be able to improve upon it.

He agreed to play his violin for them, but he hated an audience.

It is a good idea to use a comma with 'and'/'or' if the sentence is long

e.g. It had been diagnosed that Ann was allergic to a large variety of everyday substances, and anti-histamine tablets did not help her in any way.

or when there is a different subject in each clause.

EXAMPLES:

Pat went to keep-fit classes every Wednesday and looked forward to her evenings out.

Pat went to keep-fit classes, and Rita went to yoga classes.

The last example has a comma because Pat is the subject of the first part of the sentence and Rita is the subject of the second part.

Commas for asides

e.g. Mary, having pushed her way through the crowd, boarded the train.

The words included within the commas give us additional information about Mary. If we took them out, we would still have a sentence – 'Mary boarded the train.'

OTHER EXAMPLES:

Mrs Casey, our caretaker, is a remarkable woman.

Remove this and the sentence still makes sense.

Our holiday, the first one for four years, was a disaster.

The sentence still makes sense without this.

She has, to my knowledge, already been reprimanded on three occasions.

This is an aside.

In all these sentences the words within the commas are asides which give us a little more information, but they could be omitted. Such asides need commas around them to separate them from the main thrust of the sentence. The commas act like a pair of brackets showing that the words within them are less important than the rest of the sentence.

You can always test if you have used commas correctly for asides. If you remove the aside, you should still have a complete sentence.

An aside can also be placed at the beginning or end of a sentence.

EXAMPLES:

To tell you the truth, it is the first new car I have bought.

It is the first new car I have bought, to tell you the truth.

When this happens only one comma is needed instead of a pair, but the same test for the comma applies.

Using the guidelines

** Put the necessary commas in these sentences.

1 Our doctor a member of the Territorials was called up to serve in the Gulf War.

2 Our doctor the most popular in the practice is an army medical reserve.

3 Saumur with its imposing chateau is an excellent place to stay.

4 I found Norwegian although similar to both Swedish and Danish very difficult to learn.

5 Maureen who used to live near us in Corby has now moved to Northampton.

6 The sail-board which we bought when we were on holiday is too heavy for me.

7 As you know I am not used to flying.

8 Tim a previous county member now plays for our team.

9 Clive although very annoying at times is usually good-tempered and reasonable.

10 The birthday card made from recycled paper was propped against the clock.

Helpful Hints

The assistant <u>arranging the perfumes</u> is responsible for this department.

That boy <u>standing next to John</u> is Isabel's brother.

The woman <u>who came in last</u> left her umbrella behind.

The picture <u>hanging at the end of the room</u> is my favourite.

The first prize goes to the man <u>standing in front of the projector.</u>

In these sentences there are no commas. The words underlined are necessary to the meaning of each sentence; they are not additional asides. In each case the words underlined tell you which person or object is being referred to.

If you removed 'standing in front of the projector' from the last example, you would not know which man had won the prize. The same applies to all the other examples.

If an aside in a sentence is not absolutely necessary and could be omitted, then it should be marked off from the main body of the sentence with commas.

If the additional information is vital to the understanding of the sentence and cannot be omitted, no commas are needed.

Commas for sense

A comma is used to help a reader make sense of your writing. Don't over-use commas as they can split sentences into jerky parts and spoil the flow. On the other hand, if to leave out a comma would make your writing unclear you must include one.

Look at these pairs of sentences and see how commas can alter sense.

> He left us to play football. (We play football)
>
> He left us to play football. (He plays football)
>
> He knows I believe she is innocent. (I believe she is innocent)
>
> He knows I believe she is innocent. (He knows she is innocent)

** Some sentences are confusing if the commas are left out or used incorrectly. Tick the correct version in each pair below.

1 According to Sue Johnson is guilty.

 According to Sue, Johnson is guilty.

2 You will not succeed however hard you work.

 You will not succeed, however, hard you work.

3 However, I don't wish to buy one.

 However I don't wish to buy one.

4 After all the girls knew.

 After all, the girls knew.

5 In writing a comma helps the reader.

 In writing, a comma helps the reader.

6 He drove to the vet's with his girlfriend and the hamster in the cage.

 He drove to the vet's with his girlfriend, and the hamster in the cage.

7 He carried the cat, and the flowers in water into the lounge.

 He carried the cat and the flowers in water into the lounge.

Using commas

** Using all your knowledge of commas, insert them where necessary in these sentences.

1 Two of them including one aimed at the captain were intercepted.

2 Our correspondent Mark Lacey saw it all happen.

3 After the school had been declared safe the children returned to the classroom.

4 The soldier who went missing on the training mission was found unhurt.

5 Mr Kieron Stevenson a 64-year-old married man was appointed as the gardening club's new chairperson.

6 Lorries many with foreign number plates rumbled along the narrow road throughout the day making the residents' lives miserable.

7 The headmaster while sympathetic to the residents' complaints said the school's new classrooms had to be built.

8 Having prepared himself well in advance he felt relaxed.

9 "Would the lady to the right of the door please step forward."

10 That elderly man sitting on the green chair is next.

11 Yes I know who you are talking about.

12 By the way I will join you.

13 To walk under a ladder so people say is unlucky.

14 When I heard the news on the television last night I was greatly distressed.

15 I was very upset when I heard the news.

16 The cat jumped onto her lap settled himself into a comfortable position and purred contentedly.

17 He dismissed without a moment's hesitation the idea of any employees being asked to move to the firm's branch in Blackpool.

Final thoughts

▶ A comma can never replace a full stop.

▶ Learn the rules for using commas but also use your common sense.

▶ Don't over-use commas. There are established reasons for using them.

▶ Commas are used so that readers can make sense of what is written.

▶ A comma is an important punctuation point but don't worry about it unduly or it will interfere with the flow of your writing. Write first and then check for punctuation afterwards.

8
Apostrophes

What is an apostrophe?

An apostrophe is a raised comma (') which shows that a letter or letters have been omitted from a word or it is used to indicate ownership.

People often worry about using apostrophes and examiners marking English scripts complain both about the lack of apostrophes and their incorrect use. However, they should not cause any problems as there are clear guidelines and, if you understand the basic uses, they are easy to deal with.

When to use the apostrophe

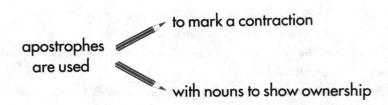

apostrophes are used

to mark a contraction

with nouns to show ownership

Apostrophes for contractions

In Chapter 4 you saw how two words were joined together and shortened to form one word.

EXAMPLES:

I'm is the shortened form of **I am**.

I'll is the shortened form of **I will/shall**.

I'd is the shortened form of **I would/should**.

I've is the shortened form of **I have**.

In each case the apostrophe is used to show that one or more letters are missing.

There are many words where this happens.

EXAMPLES:

can't (cannot)	isn't (is not)
shouldn't (should not)	aren't (are not)
wouldn't (would not)	we're (we are)
where's (where is)	he's (he is)
it's (it is)	we'll (we will/shall)
4 o'clock (4 of the clock)	sou'wester (south west gale or special rain hat)

Helpful Hints

shan't is the shortened form of shall not.

won't is the shortened form of will not.

In each of these cases the spelling of the original word changes.

An apostrophe that indicates a missing letter can also be added to a noun.

8

e.g. The washing machine's leaking.

The washing machine is leaking.

Here the 'i' of 'is' has been omitted and replaced by an apostrophe.

An apostrophe can also indicate that numbers are missing.

e.g. I was born in '62.

'19' has been replaced by an apostrophe as it is imagined that the reader will understand which century is referred to.

Using apostrophes for contractions

** Write the shortened forms of these pairs of words. Remember that the apostrophe should be placed where the letters have been omitted.

do not	I would
let us	have not
who is	did not
must not	had not
they would	they are
does not	what is

Guidance

If you are ever uncertain about writing any shortened form, think about the full version and then work out which letters you are omitting. The apostrophe will appear in the exact position of the missing letters.

Such contractions are only used in informal writing, for example, letters to friends and relatives, and when we want to record or mimic the exact words spoken by someone. Such dialogue appears in quotation marks.

e.g. "If he's going, I'm staying at home," Clare retorted.

In formal writing, shortened forms should be avoided.

e.g. Bill complained, "Well, 'e 'ardly ever 'appens to 'ave any money."

In this sentence an apostrophe appears every time Bill drops an 'h'.

When you want to write careless or rough speech, an apostrophe is used for any missing letters.

e.g. "I know, 'cos the loot's missin'," boasted Len.

Using apostrophes in dialogue

** Put in all the necessary apostrophes in this dialogue.

"Its two oclock. Well miss the train if we dont hurry," complained Mark.

"I cant find my keys. This drawers full of rubbish. Ill never find them," wailed Jane.

"Lets leave them," Mark insisted. "Weve only fifteen minutes left."

Jane shouted, "Theyre here, under the bureau! No wonder I couldnt see them."

Apostrophes to show ownership

Richard picked up the baby's toys. It was his wife's night out and he was in charge. The twins' coats were on his favourite chair, his eldest son's football kit was strewn on the table and the floor was covered in dog's hair. He would ignore the mess and read. As he picked up his book, he noticed greasy smears on the book's cover and his daughter's unmistakable signature inside the front cover.

He had suffered enough problems at work today. Three of his cashiers' calculators had disappeared, the photocopier's key had been mislaid and all the canteen assistants' overalls had shrunk at the laundry. All that had kept him going was the thought of a peaceful night's reading.

's

An 's' with an apostrophe immediately before it usually indicates that the noun to which it is attached owns something.

EXAMPLES:

baby's toys – the toys belonging to the baby

wife's night out – the night out for his wife

son's football kit – the football kit belonging to his son

dog's hair – the hair of his dog

book's cover – the cover of the book

daughter's unmistakable signature – the unmistakable signature of his daughter

photocopier's key – the key belonging to the photocopier

In each of these cases there is <u>one</u> owner.

one baby

one wife

one son

one dog

one daughter

one photocopier

An 's has been placed after the owner's name to show the reader that something is owned.

The word or words immediately following the owner's name are the items which are owned.

owner	item owned
baby	toys
wife	night out
son	football kit
dog	hair
book	cover
daughter	unmistakable signature
photocopier	key

8

If there is one owner,

> write the word for the owner,
> place an apostrophe after it, and
> add 's'.

If there is one owner, the apostrophe must go before the 's'.

s'

Look now at the words from the passage where the apostrophe appears after the 's'. Note the following instances:

twins' coats – we know when there are twins there must be two.

cashiers' calculators – we are told that the calculators of three of his cashiers
have disappeared.

assistants' overalls – we are not told how many assistants there are, but 'all'
will obviously mean more than one.

In each case there is more than one owner. The position of the apostrophe indicates this.

If there is more than one owner,

> write the word for the owners and
> place an apostrophe after it.

If there is more than one owner, the apostrophe must go after the 's'.

If you follow this simple guideline, you will be able to cope with most apostrophes for ownership.

Recognising the owner/s

** How many owners are there in each case? The position of the apostrophe gives you the answer. You need only write 'singular' or 'plural' after each of these as singular means one and plural means more than one.

1 the directors' secretaries

2 the library's entire store

3 the candidates' papers

4 the enemy's army

5 the aeroplane's fuel tank

6 the plant's roots

7 these employees' files

8 the safes' contents

9 Mike's business

10 Adele's computer

** In each of the phrases above, there is an owner or owners and some thing or things which belong to the owner. Write the words under the appropriate column. The first one has been entered as an example.

owner	owned
directors	secretaries

Helpful Hints

There are occasions when we leave out the word that is owned by the owner.

e.g. I hurried to the greengrocer's.

The word telling us what the greengrocer owned has been omitted. We do not really need 'shop' as we all know what is meant.

e.g. This evening I'm going to Hilary's.

This sentence probably refers to Hilary's home. The word 'house', 'flat' etc. has been omitted. Make certain you always include the apostrophe in such situations.

Special plurals

singular	plural
one cashier	three cashiers
one assistant	many assistants
one footballer	fifteen footballers
one engineer	ten engineers
one tree	a forest of trees

Most English words, like the ones above, end in 's' in their plural forms. So when we want to use an apostrophe to show ownership, it goes after the final 's'.

EXAMPLES:

cashiers' calculators

assistants' overalls

footballers' contracts

engineers' desks

trees' trunks

But the plural form of each of the following words is irregular. They do not end in 's'.

singular	plural
child	children
woman	women
man	men
deer	deer
salmon	salmon

When you want to use such plural words as owners,
    write the plural form,
    place an apostrophe after it and
    add an 's'.

EXAMPLES:

Children's bikes must be parked in the cycle shed.

Women's clothes are on the ground floor.

Men's clubs are very popular.

The **deer's** antlers were caught in the wire fence.

This stretch of river was the **salmon's** favourite haunt.

In the last two sentences, where the words 'salmon' and 'deer' are the same in their singular and plural forms, it is impossible to tell from an isolated sentence whether one or more creature is referred to.

singular	plural
brother-in-law	brothers-in-law
daughter-in-law	daughters-in-law

When such compound words become owners, the apostrophe is added after the last part of the word.

EXAMPLES:

My **brother-in-law's** motorbike was stolen.

Both my **brothers-in-law's** mothers are still alive.

His **daughter-in-law's** sister is staying with them.

My three **daughters-in-law's** cars are parked in my drive.

Names ending in 's'

When people's names end in 's', you can either:
write the name and put an apostrophe after it

EXAMPLES:

Giles' bedroom   **Charles'** briefcase
James' grandmother **Mrs Sykes'** employer

or write the name, put an apostrophe after it and add an 's'.

EXAMPLES:

Giles's bedroom   **Charles's** briefcase
James's grandmother **Mrs Sykes's** employer

The choice is yours.

Helpful Hints

This only applies to proper nouns. It does not apply to common nouns ending in 's' or 'ss'. Here you must obey the apostrophe guidelines.

EXAMPLES:

I shall refer to the **atlas's** index.

The jury did not believe the **witness's** story.

The **bosses'** wishes must be considered.

Possessive pronouns

The use of the apostrophe to show ownership only applies to nouns.

hers, its, ours, theirs, his and **yours** are possessive pronouns. They are words used instead of nouns and show that someone owns something.

e.g. This is Paula's handbag.

    This is **hers.** ('hers' replaces the proper noun 'Paula')

Possessive pronouns are never used with an apostrophe.

Consequently, at the end of letters,

> Yours faithfully
> Yours sincerely
> Yours affectionately

do not have apostrophes.

'One' needs an apostrophe to show ownership.

e.g. It is **one's** duty to attend. (the duty of a person)

But 'one' does not need an apostrophe when it is used as a plural.

e.g. He always chooses the **ones** with soft centres.

(plural of one)

Using apostrophes to show possession

** Insert the necessary apostrophes in these phrases and sentences.

1 the childrens responsibility

2 its paintwork

3 mens interests

4 two girls reputations

5 ones life

6 womens work

7 Yours was over there.

8 I know the ones you mean.

9 He was unaware that the car was theirs.

10 The sheeps wool was spun on the farm.

** Rewrite these sentences so that they require apostrophes.

e.g. I visited the Advice Bureau for Citizens.

I visited the Citizens' Advice Bureau.

1 She hung up the clothes of the ladies.

2 The case of the double bass had been forced open.

3 The guarantees for the presses had expired.

4 The teacher of the class was new.

5 The mother of Peter Simms lives next door to me.

6 That is the bicycle of Miss Curtis.

7 The yacht of Mr Malpass won the race.

Time

In the first passage under the heading **Ownership**, you saw the sentence:

All that had kept him going was the thought of a peaceful **night's reading**.

'night's reading' means 'a night of reading' or 'a night for reading'.

Many expressions of time require an apostrophe.

EXAMPLES:

one day's pay (payment for one day – singular)

one month's leave (leave for one month – singular)

today's menu (the menu for today – singular)

four years' imprisonment (imprisonment for four years – plural)

three weeks' holiday (a holiday of three weeks – plural)

two hours' wait (a wait of two hours – plural)

If there is one period of time, the apostrophe goes before the 's'; if the period of time is plural, the apostrophe appears after 's'.

Using apostrophes to indicate time

** Add the apostrophe to these phrases:

1 a days outing

2 in six months time

3 four days drive

4 five minutes rest

5 three months credit

6 a seconds delay

7 a years study

8 the seasons programme

9 a good nights sleep

10 five weeks marking

11 six years work

12 a lifetimes wear

13 an afternoons enjoyment

14 two years secondment

15 a terms grant

16 two years tax arrears

Common confusions

it's and its

These words cause confusion because they are written with or without an apostrophe, according to the way they are used in a sentence.

it's stands for it is. The apostrophe shows that the letter 'i' has been omitted.

its shows possession and does not need an apostrophe.

e.g. The bird injured **its** wing. (the wing belonging to the bird)

If you ever doubt which one to use, then try to replace the its/it's you have written with 'it is'. If the sentence makes sense, you want **it's**; if it doesn't make sense, you need **its**.

EXAMPLES:

The model car won't work because its/it's batteries are flat.

Try 'it is':

The model car won't work because **it is** batteries are flat.

This doesn't make sense so you need 'its'.

Sally agrees that its/it's mine.

Try 'it is':

Sally agrees that **it is** mine.

This makes sense so you need **it's**.

There's and theirs

Although these two words are spelt differently, they sound the same and can be confused.

there's is the shortened form of there is or there are.

theirs shows possession and does not need an apostrophe.

EXAMPLES:

There's egg on your jumper.

That blue car is **theirs**. (the car belongs to them)

If in doubt, test by trying to replace there's/theirs in the sentence with the words 'there is' or 'there are'. If the sentence makes sense, you need 'there's'; if it doesn't make sense, you need 'theirs'.

Who's and whose

These two words also sound alike despite the difference in spelling.

who's is the shortened form of who is or who has.

whose indicates ownership and doesn't need an apostrophe.

EXAMPLES:

Who's the man in the corner? (who is)

Who's written this on my pad? (who has)

I know **whose** shoes those are. (to whom the shoes belong)

Try the usual test if you are uncertain. Substitute **who is** or **who has** for the who's/whose word. If the sentence makes sense, you need **who's**; if not, you need **whose**.

Checking apostrophes

If you are doubtful about an apostrophe you have written, then carry out checks. Check all routes:

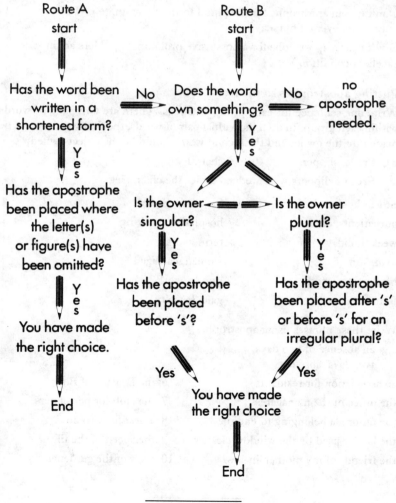

Final thoughts

▶ Use an apostrophe for contractions. (e.g. Don't....)

▶ Use an apostrophe for nouns to show ownership.

▶ Put the apostrophe before 's' if there is one owner. (e.g. ...a policeman's truncheon....)

▶ Put the apostrophe after 's' if there is more than one owner. (e.g. ...all the miners' lamps....)

▶ Irregular plurals are special cases. The apostrophe comes after the plural of the word and before the 's' that is added. (e.g. ... the children's library....)

▶ Don't use an apostrophe for the plural form of a noun. (e.g. The five judges met every Thursday.)

▶ Don't use an apostrophe for a possessive pronoun. (e.g. Hers are in excellent condition.)

Putting apostrophes to the test

** Write one sentence for each group of words. There are two pairs of words within each group. In each individual pair of words, the first word should be made into the owner and the second word should be the object owned.

e.g. Freda, slippers   chair, leg

   Freda's slippers were wedged under the chair's leg.

1 St Mark, church	St James, Street
2 outpatients, clinic	hospital, East Wing
3 week, holiday	term, work
4 man, suit	woman, cardigan
5 headmaster, study	pupils, work
6 farmer, crops	gale, ferocity

** Write these phrases using apostrophes.

e.g. an absence of two days
   two days' absence

1 an association for residents	6 the Brigade of Boys
2 the office of the manageress	7 the club for pensioners
3 the umbrella belonging to Pauline	8 a nest for a robin
4 the ladder used by the window cleaner	9 the speed of the film
5 the friends of my mother–in–law	10 tools of the gardener

** Insert the apostrophes in this extract from a conversation.

MOTHER	Id love to hear about him.
DAUGHTER	I cant think who you mean.
MOTHER	That new boyfriend of yours!
DAUGHTER	Isnt anything special to tell you.
MOTHER	Whats his job?
DAUGHTER	Hes twenty, unemployed, his names Matthew, his mothers called Sally, his pets names are Mrs P. and Mitten. Enough?
MOTHER	Ive heard he lives in that large house next to the newsagents.
DAUGHTER	So what?
MOTHER	His parents must be wealthy. Oh well, I suppose he wont be a bad lad if he comes from wealthy parents!

8

Don't let apostrophes worry you as you write. It is always best to complete a piece of writing and then go back to check for apostrophes. The more you write, the more practice you will have in using them and the more proficient you will become.

9
Conversations and Quoting

(from *How to Survive Children* by K Whitehorn)

In cartoons the actual words spoken by each character are shown in speech bubbles. In ordinary text inverted commas are placed around words to show that they are either the actual words spoken or are quotations from another piece of writing.

What are inverted commas?

They are punctuation marks and can be double "........." or single '.........'. Either is acceptable and the choice is yours. However, it is customary to use double inverted commas around speech and single inverted commas for other types of quotation.

EXAMPLES:

"I hate you," she declared. (double inverted commas around words spoken)

I have read both 'The Skull Beneath the Skin' and 'Devices and Desires'. (single inverted commas around quoted book titles)

The use of single and double inverted commas in this way allows you to indicate a quotation clearly within a passage of speech.

e.g. Ikbar said, "I hope we have time to watch 'Sportsnight' before we go out."

Inverted commas can also be referred to as 'speech' marks or 'quotation' marks. Whatever you choose to call them, these punctuation marks are used as indicators to show that words are being quoted. These words may be:

speech – dialogue, conversation, talks, lectures, etc.

quotes – from books, magazines, newspapers, letters, notices, etc.

titles – of books, newspapers, magazines, films, programmes, etc.

particular words – slang, foreign words, words used out of their normal context, etc.

When to use inverted commas

▶ for speech
▶ for other quotations

Speech

There are two ways of expressing speech in writing.

direct speech   indirect (or reported) speech

actual words   conversation
  recorded   described

Direct speech

When the actual words a speaker uses are written down, inverted commas mark them off from the rest of the text.

Example 1:

> Burden was in his shirt sleeves, a plastic apron around his waist. He took this off hurriedly when he saw who his caller was.
>
> "Just finishing the dishes," he said. "I'll nip out for some beer, shall I?"

(from Some Lie and Some Die by Ruth Rendell)

Example 2:

> "Come off it, Mr Dent," he said, "you can't win you know.
> You can't lie in front of the bulldozer indefinitely."
> He tried to make his eyes blaze fiercely but they just
> wouldn't. Arthur lay in the mud and squelched at him.
> "I'm game," he said. "We'll see who rusts first."

(from Hitch Hiker's Guide to the Galaxy by Douglas Adams)

Guidelines for the punctuation of direct speech are given later in this chapter.

Indirect (or reported) speech

Indirect speech conveys the content of the speech to the reader without repeating the actual words spoken.

Example 1:

"Your car is ready for collection," said the engineer.

In indirect speech this becomes:

The engineer said that my car was ready for collection.

The person who has spoken is identified before describing what he/she said. This is the usual pattern in indirect speech.	The word 'that' goes before the description of the speech. In indirect speech 'that' is commonly used as a link between the speaker and the described speech.	The speech account is given in the past tense. Speech is often 'moved back' into the past tense when expressed in indirect speech.

Example 2:

"We hope to arrive at Heathrow on flight BA213," Helen replied. (direct speech)

Helen replied that they hoped to arrive at Heathrow on flight BA213. (indirect speech)

We in the direct speech example has become **they** in the indirect speech example. This has happened because the viewpoint of the sentence has changed from the person actually saying the words to that of the writer who describes what has been said.

e.g. "I want to come," said Paul.

viewpoint of speaker

Paul said that he wanted to come.

viewpoint of writer

In indirect speech the writer often uses third person pronouns (**he, she** or **they**) in the speech description.

<u>Example 3</u>:

"I expected him to be here by now," replied Mrs Smith.
(direct speech)

Mrs Smith replied that she had expected him to be there by then
(indirect speech)

here and **now** in the direct speech sentence have become **there** and **then** in the indirect speech sentence. As you have already seen in <u>example 1</u>, verbs in the present tense are often moved back into the past in indirect speech.

<u>direct speech</u>	<u>indirect speech</u>
▶ actual words quoted	▶ content of speech described
▶ use inverted commas	▶ inverted commas not required
▶ speech given from viewpoint of speaker	▶ speech given from viewpoint of writer
▶ tense appropriate to situation	▶ generally past tense used
▶ speaker uses pronoun appropriate to situation	▶ third person pronoun often used
	▶ 'that' used (or implied) as a link word

Practising indirect speech

** Change these sentences from direct to indirect speech.

1 "There's been an accident," she explained.

2 "Neals are selling shoes at 50% off," said Mrs Roberts.

3 "My car," he said, "seems to have broken down."

4 "I missed the train today because my watch had stopped," replied Ian.

5 "It's not a good year for fruit," said Mr Palmer.

6 "Am I expected to work in this mess?" she asked.

7 "I haven't had a puncture for years," Carol stated.

8 "I'm not buying cheese from that shop again," Barry said. "The last lot was mouldy."

Punctuating direct speech

Direct speech may be shown in writing in various ways:

Example 1:

"Let's go out this evening," said Rozira.

    words spoken   speaker

Example 2:

He asked, "What's for dinner this evening?"

speaker   question/words spoken

Example 3:

"If you walk too far," Colin said, "you'll be exhausted."

words spoken   speaker   continuation of speech sentence

Example 4:

"The washing machine isn't working," she said. "I'll have to phone the engineer."

words spoken   speaker   second speech sentence

The words spoken are always shown within inverted commas. Words within the speech marks are separated from the rest of the sentence by a **comma, question mark** or **exclamation mark**.

EXAMPLES:

"I hope he is better " said Hugh.

"Why did you do it " questioned the policeman.

"How kind of you " she exclaimed.

When the spoken words end with a question mark or exclamation mark, no comma or full stop is required.

EXAMPLES:

"Where is it " he asked.

Neil shouted, "Don't touch "

Final punctuation marks (i.e. full stops, commas, question marks or exclamation marks) associated with the spoken words are placed inside the inverted commas.

EXAMPLES:

"It's been raining all day," she moaned.

"How are you?" asked Karl.

The first word within the speech marks always starts with a capital letter except when a sentence is interrupted.

e.g. "I hope to visit you," <u>she said</u>, "but I can't promise."

|
interruption

The first word within the speech marks following the interruption has a lower case letter.

EXAMPLES:

"Up to now," <u>Peter said</u>, "we've been lucky."

<u>interruption</u> **lower case letter**

"The battle has been won," <u>announced the general</u>, "but we must not be complacent."

<u>interruption</u>   **lower case letter**

Sometimes it is difficult to decide whether a sentence has been interrupted or whether there are in fact two sentences of speech. If you are uncertain, take out the interruption. If the sentence still makes sense, it is one sentence.

e.g. "What time," she asked, "will you be home?"

Remove 'she asked'

"What time will you be home?"

Does it make sense?

Yes

It is one sentence.

For the first letter after the interruption, use a lower case letter.

Study this example of dialogue. You will notice that each character has several sentences of speech.

> "This is great," spluttered Arthur, "this is really terrific. Let go of me you brute!"
>
> The Vogon guard dragged them on.
>
> "Don't worry," said Ford. "I'll think of something."
> He didn't sound hopeful.
>
> "Resistance is useless!" bellowed the guard.
>
> "Just don't say things like that," stammered Ford. "How can anyone maintain a positive mental attitude if you're saying things like that?"
>
> "My God," complained Arthur, "you're talking about a positive mental attitude and you haven't had your planet demolished today. I woke this morning and thought I'd have a nice relaxed day, do a bit of reading, brush the dog.... It's now just after four in the afternoon and I'm already being thrown out of an alien spaceship six light years away from the smoking remains of earth!"
>
> (from *The Hitch Hiker's Guide to the Galaxy* by Douglas Adams)

Helpful Hints

▶ Inverted commas are placed around whole groups of uninterrupted speech sentences, not around each separate sentence.

▶ A new paragraph is started each time there is a change of speaker. This helps the reader to follow the conversation.

Using the guidelines

** Insert the correct punctuation in these sentences.

1 I hope we will see you at the exhibition said the salesman

2 Jane and Val work together in the same office she said but they never speak to one another

3 Mr Holdsworth said I shall have a good crop of potatoes this year

4 Last year we visited Scotland Penny explained and we hope to visit it again this summer

5 My exam results were terrible he confessed

6 The lounge and the dining room both need decorating she said Have you any idea when you can do them

7 Well she said I am surprised

8 I see Brookside is on at 7.00 pm tonight Dorothy said I hope I'll be home in time

9 The sheep broke through a hole in the fence he explained but we've managed to get them all back

10 Will you mend it for me he asked or shall I return it to the shop

When to use direct speech

Direct speech can be useful in essays to create an authentic atmosphere. By showing the words that a person uses you can build up a clear picture of a person's character, speech mannerisms, dialect, etc. However, it is advisable only to quote direct speech if it adds to the story, as too much can slow down your narrative.

Direct speech is usually unsuitable in other formal writing tasks. It is generally preferable to summarise conversations, views or comments in formal letters and reports unless the actual words spoken have special significance.

Other quotations

Quotes from books, newspapers, notices, etc.

Example 1:

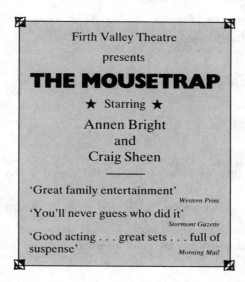

Firth Valley Theatre

presents

THE MOUSETRAP

★ Starring ★

Annen Bright
and
Craig Sheen

'Great family entertainment'
Western Print

'You'll never guess who did it'
Stormont Gazette

'Good acting . . . great sets . . . full of suspense'
Morning Mail

Each excerpt from the newspaper reviews is enclosed within inverted commas.

A book I was reading about English pubs described the Boat Inn as, 'the best inn in Britain, serving excellent food with a superb range of drinks.'

The quotation is marked off from the rest of the sentence by inverted commas.

Titles

When a title of a book, film, play or television programme is quoted within a piece of writing, it is customary to place inverted commas around it.

e.g. Last month I read 'Managing with Information Technology' to help me with the course I was studying.

When titles are listed, the commas separating the listed titles are placed outside the inverted commas. Inverted commas are placed around each individual title.

e.g. Sylvester Stallone starred in 'Rocky Two', 'Rocky Three' and 'Rocky Four'.

Particular words

Inverted commas are placed around individual words or phrases when the writer wishes to show that in some way the words are being used outside their normal context.

This occurs in the case of foreign words and phrases,

e.g. I'm 'au fait' with computers.

slang,

e.g. He threatened me with 'a bunch of fives'.

and deliberate misuse.

e.g. He 'liberated' the car.

Individual letters

When individual letters or words are quoted, they are often shown within inverted commas.

e.g. His report card showed he had been given an 'A' in history.

Unless you write essays, you won't have many opportunities to use inverted commas for quotations, but the rules for using them are quite clear and by following the guidance given in this chapter, you should feel reasonably confident about them. From time to time you may need to look back to the punctuation patterns of direct speech to refresh your memory.

Sometimes there can be a problem in identifying which words the inverted commas should enclose. If you are uncertain, try applying this checklist to your writing:

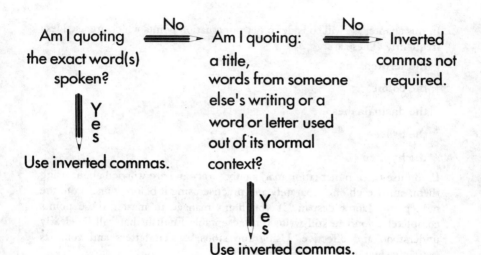

Am I quoting the exact word(s) spoken? ⟹ **No** ⟹ Am I quoting: a title, words from someone else's writing or a word or letter used out of its normal context? ⟹ **No** ⟹ Inverted commas not required.

Yes

Use inverted commas.

Yes

Use inverted commas.

9

10
Other Punctuation Points

In this chapter we will consider other punctuation points which are used less frequently. These are:

the semicolon

the colon

the dash/dashes

the brackets

the hyphen

If you use these punctuation marks only rarely and are worried about using them, study each one separately and practise using it before going on to the next point. Don't despair. If you don't manage to master these points completely, you can still write very acceptable English that will be clearly understood and effective. Using full stops, capital letters and commas correctly should be your prime concern.

As you read this chapter you will see that in some cases these punctuation points can be used instead of those you have already been introduced to. The punctuation points in this chapter allow you greater flexibility in your writing so that you can consider the effect you want to create.

A semicolon is used

▶ for closely related statements
▶ for contrast
▶ for lists

Semicolons in closely related statements

A semicolon can be used to separate two or more closely related, independent statements from one another.

Each statement must be a sentence in its own right, but the word after the semicolon does not need a capital letter unless there is a specific reason.

Example 1:

There are eleven players in a football team in rugby football there are fifteen.

Each statement either side of the semicolon is an independent sentence and could have been punctuated thus:

Example 2:

There are eleven players in a football team In rugby football there are fifteen.

Alternatively the sentence could have been written:

Example 3:

There are eleven players in a football team whereas in rugby football there are fifteen.

Why use a semicolon?

A semicolon creates a different kind of effect in your writing from a full stop or a comma.

In example 1 the reader pauses at the semicolon, but the pause is slighter than that indicated by a full stop. The semicolon allows the reader to see the close relationship between the two sentences.

In example 2 the full stop indicates a lengthier pause. The first sentence is completely separated from the second sentence.

10

In example 3 the conjunction 'whereas' links the two sentences. The comma introduces a slighter pause than in the first two examples and the effect is less dramatic.

All three examples are correct. You can choose whichever you prefer.

Good writing should include a variety of sentences of differing lengths and structures. Being able to use semicolons gives you another option. Too many short sentences separated by full stops can give your writing an abrupt and jerky effect.

Using semicolons

** Punctuate the following, using semicolons. Remember a semicolon is used to join sentences which are closely related in meaning. They may share a common subject or topic.

1 A Bactrian camel has two humps a dromedary has a single hump.

2 Kerry hesitated as she went to slam the car door she checked the keys were in her pocket.

3 I won't be home tonight I have cricket practice.

4 Her operation had to be cancelled this was a sensible decision as she had a cold.

5 The workforce walked out they could not tolerate the situation any longer.

6 He won't be going to Switzerland for his holiday this year he went there twice on business last month.

7 I am not going to the meeting tonight I have a headache.

8 Barbara's first retail job was at Sainsbury's her second was at Tesco's.

9 The golf ball hit the window it broke the glass.

10 Each day I go to college by train I could just as easily go by bus.

When you have checked your answers, you may like to go back and see if it is possible to punctuate each example in two different ways:

1 making each example into two separate sentences;

2 joining the two sentences in each example with a conjunction.

Notice the different effects you can create by using different punctuation marks.

Semicolons to show contrast

A semicolon can be used to join two sentences which indicate a sharp contrast.

EXAMPLES:

Mike enjoys winter; his wife prefers summer.

My brother loves modern art; I hate it.

Sally has masses of dark curly hair; her son's hair is blond and straight.

Semicolons for lists

You have already practised using commas in lists. Semicolons are sometimes preferable in a long, complicated list which may already contain commas.

EXAMPLES:

The room was full of activities: children painting posters, banners and friezes; mothers sewing cloaks, curtains and bonnets.

The sports complex has excellent facilities: a swimming pool with a flume; a well-equipped multi-gym; a supervised play area for the under-fives; an indoor five-a-side pitch.

There are many reasons for Joe's appalling behaviour: his parents, although they always did their best, had never made him respect property; the school, recommended by his aunt, had a lax attitude to discipline; and finally, according to Terry, Joe enjoyed being in trouble.

If commas had been used in these lists to separate the main items from one another, the reader would have been confused. Semicolons make the divisions in the lists clearer. They visually separate one item from the next.

More semicolon practice

** Punctuate these lists with commas and semicolons. It helps if you identify each main item first.

1 I have been sent to collect the following items: the Olivetti word processor with the built-in printer the computer desk delivered last week a box of fifty discs ordered from Rapid Foreward two printer covers discarded by the legal department and a set of encyclopaedias.

2 Winter had arrived early that year: the drive had been a sheet of glistening ice for the past month the ancient plumbing system although its pipes had been wrapped in sacking had completely frozen each morning the insides of the windows were encrusted in ice and for days they had been without electricity.

Colons are used

▶ for lists
▶ for speech and quotations
▶ to explain, expand and summarise

Colons for lists

You are probably well aware of the commonest use of the colon – to introduce a list. If you look back to sentences 1 and 2 above, you will see that each list is introduced by a colon.

The colon indicates to the reader that something will follow.

You use it if you want your reader to pause before reading the list. It is not necessary to use a dash after the colon (:-); the colon is sufficient on its own. A capital letter is not needed after a colon except for a specific purpose.

EXAMPLES:

I have seen several plays at the Repertory Theatre recently 'Anthony and Cleopatra', 'Saturday, Sunday, Monday', 'Cider with Rosie' and 'Translations'.

I disapproved of three aspects of his lecture his incorrect reference to York, the poor quality of his slides and his loud, booming voice.

10

Using colons in lists

** Insert colons to introduce these lists.

1 There was a variety of vehicles in his drive a caravan, a vintage car, a classic motorbike and a brand new Rolls Royce.

2 We visited four counties in all Lancashire, Yorkshire, Durham and Northumberland.

3 She read three books during the Christmas holiday 'The Naked Ape', '500 Mile Walkies' and 'Spycatcher'.

4 He applied to four universities Cardiff, Kent, Leicester and Surrey.

5 "Which floor would you like toys, furnishings or ladies' fashions?"

Colons for speech and quotations

A colon can be used to introduce a passage of direct speech or a quotation, but it is more usual to use a comma.

EXAMPLES:

He rolled on the floor shouting "Fetch the doctor immediately."

In your previous essay you stated 'Gladstone was less effective in Ireland than Disraeli'.

Colons to explain, expand, summarise

A colon is often used to divide one part of a sentence from another when the second half explains, expands or summarises the first half.

EXAMPLES:

My life has changed I have a job, a house, a family.

I am certain of one thing I will attend the interview.

One example of his unreliability was seen last week his absence from the briefing meeting.

Here the colon is again used to indicate that something will follow – an example, an explanation or a summary.

You can check if you have used a colon for the correct reason if you think of the colon standing for 'namely'.

e.g. I sat down to eat my tea: the telephone rang.

The two statements in this sentence are about different subjects and do not depend upon one another. The 'telephone rang' does not explain, expand or summarise 'eating my tea'. The 'namely' test does not work.

e.g. There was only one answer: find a job.

'find a job' explains the first part of the sentence. The 'namely' test works.

More colon practice

** Use colons correctly in these sentences.

1 Shuffling the papers together, he came to a decision he'd resign.

2 The birds scattered they must have heard the cat.

3 The weather is the same every day hot, dry and windy.

4 It was his most successful day so far he had sold three cars.

5 Stella was bitterly disappointed she had failed her driving test.

6 Bradley knew what he must do marry her.

7 The young man had only one thought revenge.

Dashes

People often pepper their writing with dashes, using them instead of other punctuation marks. They should not be used to add on extra pieces of information to a sentence at random. They have specific uses and can be very effective when used correctly.

A single dash

A single dash can be used near the end of a sentence to indicate:

▶ a dramatic pause

▶ an explanation

▶ an interrupted conversation

A dramatic pause

e.g. "They have been found – alive!"

The dash makes the reader pause so that the single word 'alive' has a greater impact. If the statement had been written without a dash, the statement would have caused less surprise and drama.

Read these sentences aloud to illustrate the effect the dash can have.

I thought I was the only one in the room – until Rex pounced.

His work was untidy and messy – yet effective.

She reached for the vase – crash!

An explanation

A dash can be used to introduce an explanation.

e.g. These are the jewels   jewels which should have been recovered years
    ago.

The part of the sentence following the dash gives more information about the
jewels.

Read these sentences and notice how the dash, in each case, is followed by an
explanation.

> The society has several functions – to provide entertainment, to support
> the residents' families and to raise money for the sheltered housing
> scheme.

> I enjoy my holidays – skiing, sailing, walking and cycling.

> He chose Bill for one reason only – he could sing.

Using the single dash

** Place a dash in each of these sentences. It may help to read each sentence
aloud, pausing where you feel the dash should go so you can check that the
remainder of the sentence forms an explanation.

1 I know now why I dislike Sue she's dishonest.

2 History, geography, English, and religious education these were his
favourite subjects.

3 We cleared the snow from the shared drive the neighbours stayed indoors.

4 I'll mend it for you when I'm ready.

The dash has the effect of drawing the reader's attention to the explanation.
As you will have seen, a colon can be used in the same way.

Dialogue

A dash marks hesitation in dialogue or an unfinished statement.

EXAMPLES:

"I know   I'm sorry   forgive me   I forgot."

"I would have come but   "

A pair of dashes

**Used in pairs, dashes allow you to separate asides, afterthoughts,
opinions or non-essential information from the main thrust of the
sentence.**

Used in this way, their function is similar to that of a pair of commas or
brackets.

EXAMPLES:

I've stopped having sugar in drinks   I was never given it as a child   and I now enjoy the taste of unsweetened tea and coffee.

He is   to be quite candid   a liar.

Guidance

It is perhaps a good idea to visualise how dashes will look on the page.

<u>Sentence 1</u> I wonder, to be quite honest, if he is suitable.

<u>Sentence 2</u> I think – I'm sorry to say this – he's a thief.

<u>Sentence 3</u> Adjectives (describing words) make writing more vivid.

At a glance, commas are not so instantly visible as dashes or brackets so the aside within the commas in <u>sentence 1</u> seems to be less separated from the sentence.

The dashes in <u>sentence 2</u> have the effect of giving the aside more prominence and so the flow of the sentence is interrupted to a greater extent.

In <u>sentence 3</u> the brackets are immediately noticeable and seem to cut off the words within them from the rest of the sentence. These bracketed words assume less importance.

So think of the effect you want to create in your writing.

▶ If you have an aside that you want to be considered, use a pair of commas.

▶ If you want your reader to pause before and after the aside to digest it, use a pair of dashes.

▶ If, however, the aside is merely touched upon briefly, use brackets.

Using a pair of dashes

** Insert a pair of dashes in each of these sentences.

1 When Petronia returned home it was later than usual the suitcase was missing.

2 I saw that film the last film to be shown there at the Classic Theatre.

3 Last September I was on holiday in France at the time my car was broken into.

4 The whole school pupils, staff, caretakers, ancillary workers joined in the the protest.

5 Your son's work as I said at our last meeting is careless and inadequate.

6 My car a luxury model when it was new now seems very uncomfortable and basic.

10

7 I understand your feelings the same thing happened to me but you must try to forget it.

8 As soon as he was promoted he had applied for the post three times he took the entire section to the pub.

9 Thousands of residents will be taking part in the National Census set for April 21 and the results will be used to plan development in the area.

10 I can understand your protesting I would if I lived where you do but I feel it will be quite futile.

Remember you can write quite adequately without recourse to dashes if you fully understand the punctuation marks in the previous chapters. Knowing about dashes allows you to create additional effects.

Brackets

As you will have already seen, brackets can be used in the same way as a pair of dashes. They divide an additional fact, explanation, comment or afterthought from the rest of the sentence and show the reader that the words within them are of secondary importance. The sentence still makes complete sense when the words within the brackets are removed.

The first word within the brackets does not need a capital letter in this position except for a specific reason. A full stop is not needed at the end of the bracketed comment either.

Don't use too many sets of brackets as they interrupt the flow of the sentence and distract the reader from the main message.

Using brackets

** Look carefully at each sentence and write a list of the occasions when brackets are useful.

1 Oliver Cromwell (1599–1658) was a distinguished soldier.

2 The room measured 3ft (0.9m) by 4ft (1.2m).

3 They visited the nearest town (55 miles away) once a month.

4 You can visit the site any Thursday between February and October (the key is at the gatehouse).

5 Take the Portsmouth road (A27) out of Southampton.

6 All details are shown on the map (page 26).

7 The fort at Caerleon (Gwent) is 3 miles (5 kilometres) north-east of Newport.

8 She arrived in a showy evening dress (typical of her) which made all heads turn.

Hyphens

Hyphens are not, strictly speaking, punctuation marks as they join words together and do not help to punctuate a sentence. A hyphen resembles a dash but the two marks should not be confused. A dash is a punctuation mark which separates groups of words within a sentence, whereas a hyphen links words together.

EXAMPLES:

plate-glass door

light-headed

pent-up emotions

Hyphens for joining words

A hyphen can be used to indicate that the rest of a word will appear on the next line.

e.g. At my local tourist office I found some information about Gloucester shire.

Guidance

Always split the word between two syllables.

EXAMPLES:

Re-member or remem-ber, never reme-mber or any other such split.

Main-tenance or mainten-ance – no other split would be acceptable here.

Put the hyphen at the end of the line – not at the beginning of the next one. Don't split one-syllable words.

EXAMPLES:

co-me

w-hat

whe-n

Avoid splitting words whenever possible. It is better to calculate the exact space needed and begin the word on the next line.

Hyphens for spelling

Hyphens are sometimes used to join two or more words to make a compound word.

EXAMPLES:

daughter-in-law	cul-de-sac
all-time record	board-game
closing-time	boat-builder
ex-captain	post-bus
self-help	hair-do
ring-road	river-bank

Hyphenated words are really the in-between stage in the evolution of words. Words that are now hyphenated started off as two distinct words. As they were frequently used together, a hyphen was used to link them. Eventually they will be written as one word.

This process has already been completed in many compound words.

EXAMPLES:

shopkeeper	playboy	handclap
hairdresser	bedroom	bookcase
sunshine	breakfast	newsagent

Hyphenated words can cause people problems as they are often uncertain when to include them. It is a complicated situation and there is no clear guidance. To add to the confusion, some words can be written in either form.

e.g.   self confidence

self-confidence

Some words which begin with a prefix need a hyphen.

EXAMPLES:

co-ordinate	re-educate
multi-national	pre-eminent
semi-precious	non-essential
pro-American	ex-husband

This can be confusing as for a particular prefix some words may have the prefix followed by a hyphen, while others will have the prefix and the word joined together without a hyphen.

EXAMPLES:

multicoloured	co-agent	pre-school
multi-ownership	coalition	preamble

A hyphen frequently occurs when a prefix ends in a vowel and the word begins with a vowel. The hyphen separates the two vowel sounds.

EXAMPLES:

co-author   pre-empt

Guidance

If you are uncertain, write the word in three ways so that you can see which version looks correct.

EXAMPLES:

washup	wristwatch
wash-up	wrist-watch ✔
wash up ✔	wrist watch
nonstick	gardencentre
non-stick ✔	garden-centre
non stick	garden centre ✔

It is often difficult to judge. You can usually tell if the two words should not be written as one, but it may be more difficult to choose between the hyphenated version and the two individual words.

If you are unsure, use your dictionary. You will need to look very carefully as some dictionaries don't make it particularly clear.

Hyphens for sense

Use your common sense to decide whether two closely connected words require a hyphen. If the sense is not clear without a hyphen then one should be included.

EXAMPLES:

He carried the red hot plate.✗
He carried the red-hot plate.✔

She attended a top level meeting.✗
She attended a top-level meeting.✔

The salesman extolled the virtues of the five door car.✗
The salesman extolled the virtues of the five-door car.✔

10

The green fingered children won the prize.✗
The green-fingered children won the prize.✔

Correct usage

** Read the following pairs of sentences and tick the correct version within each pair. Use the clues in brackets to help you.

1 Bradley plays on the right wing.
                              (the position)
  Bradley plays on the right-wing.

2 Our boss has left wing tendencies.
                              (his politics)
  Our boss has left-wing tendencies.

3 The top heavy basket fell over.
                              (unevenly loaded)
  The top-heavy basket fell over.

4 It was a hair raising event.
                              (very frightening)
  It was a hair-raising event.

5 Peter was a hard working man.
                              (works very hard)
  Peter was a hard-working man

Helpful Hints

▶ Use hyphens sensibly.

▶ Don't use them unnecessarily.

▶ If two closely connected words in a sentence make sense as separate units, write them without a hyphen.

Summary

▶ A **semicolon** can:

      link two closely related sentences into one longer sentence

      join sentences which indicate a contrast

      be used in a long or complicated list

▶ A **colon** can:

>   introduce a list
>
>   introduce dialogue or a quotation
>
>   introduce an explanation or summary

▶ A **single dash** can:

>   introduce a dramatic pause
>
>   introduce an explanation
>
>   mark a hesitation or unfinished statement

▶ A **pair of dashes** marks an aside.

▶ **Brackets** are used for less important asides.

▶ A **hyphen** links two or more closely related words together.

Final thoughts

Semicolons, colons, dashes and hyphens, when used correctly, can make your writing more exact. If you still lack confidence in using them, don't worry; you can write very good English without them. Look at well-written books, newspapers and magazines and see how these punctuation marks are used. By noticing how others use them, you will gradually become more familiar with their use.

10

To Sum Up

In this section you have been introduced to the main punctuation points. Although we have tried to introduce them in order of complexity and frequency, it is often difficult to separate one mark from another. The most important aspects of good punctuation are being able to write in sentences and use capital letters for the right reasons. Master these fundamental skills and then concentrate on the other punctuation marks.

Write as much as possible and for as many reasons as possible so that you need to use a wide range of punctuation. By using punctuation marks, you will become more confident. Gradually you will begin to use them automatically without worrying about them.

Be alert when you are reading and notice how others punctuate their writing. Analyse why a certain punctuation mark has been used. If you are in doubt, go back over a particular chapter or section within it again. Don't try to learn too much at a time, but take it in small steps so that you have time to digest and practise one skill before moving on to the next.

Punctuation is important when writing, but concentrate on content first and then check your punctuation afterwards. Punctuation is one of the writer's tools which enables a reader to understand the written word.

Paragraphs also help your reader to understand your writing. A paragraph is a group of sentences about a topic. When a new topic is developed, a new paragraph is needed. Paragraphs can be any length, but very long paragraphs can cause confusion and very short paragraphs can give your writing a jerky effect. Ideally your writing should contain a variety of paragraphs of differing lengths. By dividing your writing into paragraphs, the reader will know when he or she is moving from one theme to another.

It is a good idea to include a 'key' sentence either as the first sentence or near the beginning of the paragraph. This key sentence should introduce the theme of the paragraph and the rest of the sentences that follow will develop the theme. The key sentence provides a signpost for the reader and helps him or her to pinpoint the theme and understand its development.

Look at a quality newspaper or novel and try to understand why the writer has chosen to begin a new paragraph. See if you can identify the key sentence in each paragraph. If you feel uncertain about paragraphs, complete your piece of writing then go back and check where each paragraph should begin. Ask yourself if you are moving on to a new aspect of the subject you are writing about. It may help if you plan your writing first. Make a list of all the pieces of information you want to include in your writing and then number them so that they are in a logical order. Each new idea will then probably form a new paragraph. The more you write, the more confident you will become about using paragraphs.

11
Introducing Grammar

In this section we will consider grammar in relation to its function in writing and speech. We will concentrate on the practice, not the study of grammar.

What is grammar?

Grammar is the system of rules which cover the way words are used and grouped together. In any language there has to be an accepted order so that we can understand one another. We all have to follow the same set of rules. A group of words is meaningless unless the conventions are followed.

e.g. He stopped snow the when to intended go out.

Although we know the meanings of all these words, we cannot derive any sense from them because they are not arranged in an accepted order. If we tried to unravel them, we may put certain words together. 'He stopped' sounds possible; 'to go out' makes sense; 'the when' would never appear in a sentence – 'when the' is far more acceptable.

By using the knowledge of English grammar we acquired as we learnt to speak – and later to read and write, we can gradually begin to make sense of these words. We might come up with:

He intended to go out when the snow stopped.

or

When the snow stopped, he intended to go out.

In Chapters 2 and 3 we considered what constituted a sentence. It is a group of words which forms a complete unit of sense. A capital letter is needed at the beginning; a full stop, question mark or exclamation mark is required at the end. Sometimes other punctuation marks are needed to help us understand the exact meaning. Correct punctuation alone is insufficient. A sentence is made up of grammatical elements and so the words within the sentence must appear in the accepted order for it to be a unit of sense. Thus grammar and punctuation go hand in hand.

How do we learn grammar?

As children, we subconsciously acquire knowlege of grammatical rules by listening to adults speaking and by imitating them. Often children misrepresent what they hear and have to be corrected.

e.g. "Me go bed."

The child would probably be told to say, "I am going to bed." With repeated practice, the correct version would be learnt. Obviously bad habits develop as well as good habits according to the 'models' we copy and whether or not we are corrected.

Even if we have never formally learnt a subject called 'grammar', we have been using it to form sentences since we were children. By talking, reading and writing, we absorb its conventions.

We may also acquire the grammar of a second language, either by learning it formally, or informally by living in a foreign country, where we imitate the speech of its inhabitants. There are often great differences between the grammar of one language and another. The grammar of any language is a matter of rules which have evolved and been accepted by its society. Much of English grammar is derived from Latin.

Grammar for different purposes

The grammar of speech and writing is the same, but because our tones of voice, gestures and facial expressions all help us to get our messages across, we can afford to be less grammatically precise when speaking. Unless we are in a very formal situation, our listeners don't expect us to use perfect grammar. However, when we express ourselves in writing, we need to know the correct grammatical structures so that our message is clear and unambiguous. In formal writing poor grammar can let us down.

Writing involves many skills. If we understand grammatical structures and use them correctly, it does not follow that we will be able to produce exact, interesting, faultless writing. Grammar is only one of the writing skills which needs to take its place alongside the other competences, nevertheless it is a considerable skill. Being at home with grammar rules can make us more confident about the writing process.

Why we need to learn grammar

▶ Grammar enables us to speak correctly and exactly when a formal situation demands a high standard.

▶ By using correct grammar structures in writing, we can deliver our messages accurately and unambiguously.

▶ Grammar helps us to understand what we are doing with language and why we are doing it.

▶ If we appreciate the grammar of our own language and understand the function of words, we can transfer these skills to learning the grammar of a foreign language.

What is correct grammar?

Correct grammar is often considered to be the language spoken by educated people: standard English. Everyone's language is unique but it has to conform to current, accepted grammatical standards. Without some kind of standardisation, communication breaks down.

Grammar is not something that is fixed for all time; the grammar of any living language slowly changes. There can be an in-between stage where two or more forms exist side by side until one takes precedence over the other.

Understanding grammar

You probably use many grammatical conventions automatically without being aware of them. There may be others that you misuse and these are the ones that you will need to make a conscious effort to learn.

Words can be divided into categories according to their functions in sentences. A word can often perform one function in one sentence and another function in a different sentence. These word categories are often called **parts of speech** and can be listed as follows:

> **nouns**
>
> **pronouns**
>
> **verbs**
>
> **adjectives**
>
> **adverbs**
>
> **prepositions**

When you look up a word in a good dictionary, you will see that its part of speech is given.

e.g. **handsome**, (adj.) good-looking: well-proportioned: dignified: liberal or noble: generous: ample. – (adv.) **handsomely.** – (n.) **handsomeness.**

(from Chambers Concise Dictrionary)

Knowing the function the word performs will help you to use the word correctly.

Chapters 12–17 look at each of the word categories in turn and consider the work each word category performs in sentences. Throughout these chapters, the emphasis is on the sentence as a unit of sense and the functions played by the words within it. By understanding the function of words, you should acquire a greater understanding of the mechanics of the language and feel more confident about writing freely and correctly.

Section 2

11

12
Nouns

A noun names a person or thing.

EXAMPLES:

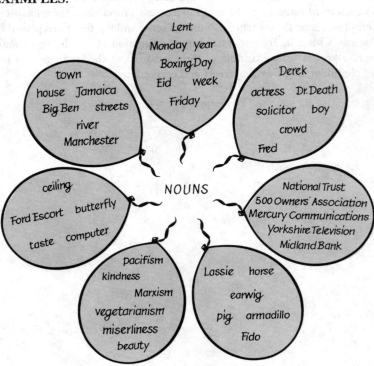

town
house Jamaica
Big Ben streets
river
Manchester

Lent
Monday year
Boxing Day
Eid week
Friday

Derek
actress Dr. Death
solicitor boy
crowd
Fred

ceiling
Ford Escort butterfly
taste computer

NOUNS

National Trust
500 Owners' Association
Mercury Communications
Yorkshire Television
Midland Bank

pacifism
kindness
Marxism
vegetarianism
miserliness
beauty

Lassie horse
earwig
pig armadillo
Fido

Nouns in sentences

▶ Nouns as subjects
▶ Nouns as objects

Nouns as subjects

In Chapters 2 and 3 you saw that a sentence must make sense and contains a verb and a subject. The subject of a sentence is the person or thing that the sentence is about.

EXAMPLES:

Carol had a terrible cold.

the subject

The fox was chased by the hounds for five miles.

the subject

The poverty was terrible to witness.

the subject

In each of these examples the subject of the sentence is a noun.

A noun can be the subject of a sentence. The subject of a sentence carries out the action in the sentence.

(See also Chapter 14. Pronouns can also be the subject of sentences: see Chapter 13.)

The subject of a sentence may be more than one person or thing.

EXAMPLES:

The crowd shouted and cheered.

the subject

Jill and Alison worked hard.

the subject

The books fell off the shelf.

the subject

As you saw in Chapter 2, the ability to write in sentences is an important skill. By being able to recognise nouns as subjects of sentences, you will increase your understanding of sentence construction and your ability to check whether you are writing in sentences. In later pages of this chapter you will be shown the various types of nouns. This information should help you to apply the sentence checklist on page 19 (Chapter 2) more effectively.

Nouns as objects

A noun can be the object of a sentence. An object is the person or thing that an action is carried out upon.

EXAMPLES:

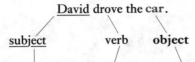

David drove the car.

subject   verb   object

does the action   **has the action done to it**

The rain filled the gutters.

subject   verb   **object**

Although every sentence has a subject or an implied subject, not every sentence contains an object.

EXAMPLES:

The dog barked.

The telephone was ringing.

Identifying nouns

** Find the nouns in these sentences.

1 Their house is by the lake.

2 The company announced a fall in its profits.

3 Her typewriter must be repaired.

4 The mountaineer fell.

5 The 6.05 train stopped at the platform.

6 His watch was very expensive.

7 The people pushed through the doors.

8 The tape became jammed in my bag.

9 Her mother visited the village.

A or an?

Sometimes the decision whether to use 'a' or 'an' before a noun can create a dilemma for the writer.

Use a before a noun which starts with:

a consonant	a long 'u' sound
EXAMPLES:	**EXAMPLES:**
a biscuit	a unit
a wheelbarrow	a union

Use **an** before a noun which starts with:

a vowel (except a long 'u' sound)

EXAMPLES:
an encyclopaedia
an optician

a silent 'h' which makes the word
sound as if it is beginning with a vowel

EXAMPLES:
an hour
an honour

Types of nouns

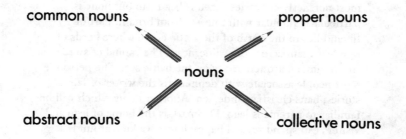

Proper nouns

These are the particular names of

people	animals	buildings/places	months/days/festivals
Jesse Jackson	Garfield	Athens	November
Archbishop Tutu	Tigger	Caernarvon Castle	Saturday
Tarzan	Snoopy	River Sowe	Yom Kippur
Charles Bradshaw	Shergar	Helvellyn	Ramadan
Betty	Bruno	Lake Ontario	Epiphany

companies/institutions	others
Marconi	Concorde (aeroplane)
Department of Trade and Industry	SS Great Britian (ship)
European Economic Community	Union Jack (Flag)
Letts Educational Ltd	Flying Scotsman (train)
Economic Development Unit	Spinning Jenny (machine)

Recognising proper nouns

** Look back to the examples of nouns given at the beginning of this chapter and underline the proper nouns within each group.

Proper nouns always have a capital letter at the beginning of each word (see Chapter 4). Because a proper noun names a particular person, place, etc., it is rare for the word to be plural.

Proper nouns in context

** Identify the proper nouns in this passage and give each of them a capital letter. The capital letter for the beginning of each sentence has already been given.

> Finland, sweden, norway and denmark are four of europe's most northerly countries. Each is beautiful but none is particularly popular with tourists from britain. Part of finland lies to the north of the arctic circle where herds of reindeer roam across the wilderness. The capital of sweden is stockholm, an attractive city on the baltic sea. The person most people associate with denmark is the writer of fairy stories, hans christian andersen. Another name which will be familiar to parents is lego. Denmark is the home of lego and visitors can spend several happy hours walking around legoland.

Common nouns

These are the general names of people, animals, places and things.

EXAMPLES:

shoe

butterfly   airport

traffic   oak   woman

window   caravan

bachelor

Common nouns name a kind or type, but not a particular person, animal, place or thing. However, some nouns can be proper or common nouns depending on the way they are used.

Example 1:

I walked along the road.

common noun

I walked along Dewhurst Road.

proper noun

Example 2:

We will meet you in the town.

He works in a city. ——————— common nouns

Luton Town football team played Manchester City

proper nouns

Common nouns may be:

singular *or* plural.

(one person, animal place, thing) | (more than one person, animal, place, thing)

EXAMPLES:

singular	plural
bird	birds
barrister	barristers
church	churches
knife	knives
jockey	jockeys
potato	potatoes
woman	women

As you can see, in the plural form of the noun an 's' is usually added, but other rules apply as well. The spelling book in this *Getting to Grips* series explains these rules.

Confusing singular and plural forms

A few common nouns appear to be plural but are classified as singular and so need a singular verb.

EXAMPLES:

The news is bad.

noun	singular verb

Measles is a nasty illness.

noun	singular verb

Some common nouns are only used in the plural and need a plural verb.

EXAMPLES:

His new trousers were on the hanger.

The scissors are blunt.

In each of these examples only one item is being referred to, but it is made up of two parts so we always use the plural form.

OTHER EXAMPLES:

glasses	secateurs	knickers
tights	scales	pyjamas

Masculine and feminine

There are a few common nouns which have a specifically masculine or feminine form.

EXAMPLES:

male	female
bachelor	spinster
boy	girl
nephew	niece
boar	sow
drake	duck
bull	cow

Suffixes are added to other nouns to show whether they are masculine or feminine.

EXAMPLES:

male	female	suffix
hero	heroine	ine
mayor	mayoress	ess
actor	actress	ess (note 'o' omitted in 'actress')
host	hostess	ess

Many nouns have one word for both male and female.

EXAMPLES:

parent	cousin
dancer	nurse

If we wish to make clear the sex of the person in such instances, we can put the words 'male' or 'female' before the noun.

e.g. The hospital employs fifty male nurses.

Abstract nouns

As the word abstract suggests, these nouns name qualities, feelings or ideas, all of which are intangible.

EXAMPLES:

hunger

equality

bitterness

cruelty

rage

faithfulness

kindness

security

Many abstract nouns end in 'ty' or 'ness' as the examples show. Other endings are also possible.

EXAMPLES:

mercy	admiration		freedom
horror	pacifism	satisfaction	hardship

12

Collective nouns

These nouns name a complete set or group of people, animals or things.

EXAMPLES:

choir	a group of singers
swarm	a group of insects
army	a group of soldiers
herd	a group of animals
library	a group of books
party	a group of people
family	a group of related people

Singular or plural?

While collective nouns consist of a number of people, animals or things, they are generally considered to be a single unit so are used in the singular.

EXAMPLES:

The choir is singing.

collective noun   singular verb

The army will be fighting its first battle.

collective noun   singular pronoun

However, when the emphasis of the sentence is on the individual members of the group, the collective noun is used in the plural sense. The supporting verb and pronoun must be used in their plural forms.

e.g. The choir are travelling here in their cars.

    plural verb   plural pronoun

(i.e. each member will come in his or her own car)

Word building with nouns

When you look up a word in a good dictionary, the part of speech is indicated. Such information will help you to use an unfamiliar word in a sentence.

> **liger**, n. cross between a lion and female tiger.

> (from *Chambers Concise Dictionary*)

Using the dictionary definition and the fact that you have been told that 'liger' is a noun, you could make a reasonable attempt at using it in a sentence.

e.g. The liger lay under the tree out of the fierce heat.

A dictionary will often give you other nouns that can be made from the root word by the addition of prefixes and suffixes.

e.g. library – noun (root word);
    librarian – noun;
    librarianship – noun.

** Using a dictionary, find other nouns that can be made from these words:

home	foot
jewel	man
hand	match
book	head

Final thoughts

In this chapter we have shown you the various types of nouns in order to help you to recognise nouns in sentences and appreciate their functions. It isn't necessary to learn the names of the various categories but by increasing your understanding of nouns and your awareness of sentence structure you should feel more confident about your writing.

Section 2

12

13
Pronouns

What is a pronoun?

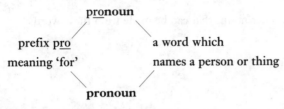

pronoun

prefix pro
meaning 'for'

a word which
names a person or thing

pronoun

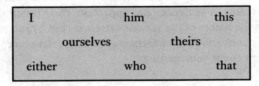

A pronoun is a word which is used instead of a noun.

All of these words can be used as pronouns:

I	him	this
ourselves		theirs
either	who	that

We use pronouns to refer to a person or thing which we have already mentioned by name. Pronouns are useful as they save us from repeating a noun. Indeed, our writing would be boring and our speech contrived if we didn't use pronouns.

EXAMPLES:

Harry and Wendy live in a flat in Sidcup which <u>Harry and Wendy</u> have rented from <u>Harry and Wendy's</u> friends.

Neil said, "Hello, Alison. How is <u>Alison</u>? <u>Neil</u> hopes <u>Alison</u> is feeling better."

If some of these proper nouns were replaced by pronouns, the sentences would sound far more natural.

Harry and Wendy live in a flat in Sidcup which they rent from their friends.

Neil said, "Hello, Alison. How are you? I hope you are feeling better."

Types of pronouns

Pronouns can be divided into categories. It doesn't matter if you don't remember the name of each type of pronoun, but it is important that you understand the work each does in a sentence. It is more convenient to look at them in groups: knowledge about types of pronouns is useful if you wish to study English or foreign languages in detail.

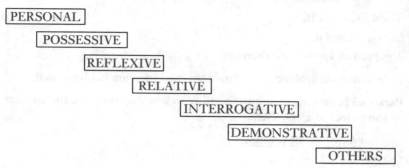

PERSONAL

POSSESSIVE

REFLEXIVE

RELATIVE

INTERROGATIVE

DEMONSTRATIVE

OTHERS

Personal pronouns

I	you	he	she	it	we	they
me		him	her		us	them

We use most of these pronouns to refer to ourselves, other people or animals.

▶ **it** is used to refer to a thing or animal.

▶ **they** can be used for people or things.

▶ **you** can be used as a singular or plural pronoun.
It can refer to one person or more than one person.

EXAMPLES:

I go for a walk.

You are standing on my toes.

He hopes to join the tennis club.

She feels unwell.

It injured its paw.

You are all guilty.

They demand an apology.

In each of these sentences the personal pronoun is the **subject** of the sentence.

In each of the following sentences the personal pronoun is the **object**. What do you notice about the personal pronouns?

Brian dislikes **me**.

Nick will help **you**.

The manager praised **him**.

The nurse comforted **her**.

The doctor read **it**.

Martyn visited **us**.

A policeman approached **them**.

In several of the sentences a different personal pronoun has been used.

Personal pronouns change according to whether they are the subject or the object of a sentence.

subject form	object form
I	me
you	you
he	him
she	her
it	it
we	us
they	them

You will notice that 'you' and 'it' remain the same regardless of whether they are used as the subject or object of a sentence.

Personal pronouns with prepositions

The object form of each personal pronoun is used when a personal pronoun follows a preposition. (There is more about prepositions in Chapter 17.)

e.g. I received a letter <u>from</u> him.

preposition   **object form of personal pronoun**

EXAMPLES:

I wrote **to her** yesterday.

He threw a stone **at me**.

The dog rushed **between us**.

The cat snuggled **against me**.

The verb 'to be'

The verb 'to be' is special as, unlike other verbs, it does not take an object so any pronoun following it should be in its subject form.

EXAMPLES:

It is I.

It is they.

Although these are grammatically correct, we are more familiar with:

It is me.

It is them.

These expressions are commonly used and are widely accepted but, when we want to use the verb 'to be' as part of a longer sentence, we should use the subject form of the personal pronoun.

EXAMPLES:

I'm afraid it's I who boiled the kettle dry.

It's they who are to blame.

Avoiding mistakes

EXAMPLES:

The policeman told the man his breath test was negative. (Whose test?)

Carol asked her aunt if she could answer the door. (Who will answer the door?)

When they saw their friends, they waved. (Who waved?)

Using a personal pronoun in a sentence can cause confusion so be careful.

EXAMPLES:

Christina will meet Tony and I outside the cinema. ✗

Christina will meet Tony and me outside the cinema. ✔

He stood next to Martin and I in the queue. ✗

He stood next to Martin and me in the queue. ✔

It is a common mistake to use 'I' instead of 'me' in such sentences. If you are uncertain whether 'I' or 'me' is appropriate, check by removing the other person's name.

e.g. He stood next to I in the queue.

You can see immediately that 'I' is wrong – 'me' is correct.

Remember, it is polite and correct to mention other people before yourself.

e.g. I and my brother will join you.✗

My brother and I will join you.✔

An extra pronoun

One can be used as an impersonal pronoun. We use it to refer to people in general instead of using 'I', 'you' or 'we'. It is very formal and should not be over-used.

It can sound very clumsy.

e.g. **One** knows **one** should be doing as **one** is told but **one** hates being ordered around.

If you begin by using 'one' in a sentence, you should not complete the sentence by using a personal pronoun.

e.g. **One** always tries to do what he can in the circumstances.✗

When 'one' is used to show ownership, it needs an apostrophe (see page 78).

e.g. I consider it to be **one's** duty to accept.

Using personal pronouns

** Replace each of the underlined word or words with a single pronoun.

1 He shared it between Liz and <u>Keith</u>.

2 Glenn begged, "Please come to stay with Helen and <u>Glenn</u>."

3 The college was threatened with closure, but <u>the college</u> has been given six months' reprieve.

4 "It's <u>Kate</u> you should ask," protested Tim.

5 <u>Judith and Janet</u> boycotted the meeting.

6 It is <u>Terry and John</u> who should be concerned about <u>Thomas</u>.

Possessive pronouns

mine   yours   his   its   ours   theirs

These are used to show ownership.

EXAMPLES:

This book is **hers**.

That briefcase is **mine**.

Ours is at the end of the row.

No apostrophes are needed with possessive pronouns.

Reflexive pronouns

| myself | yourself | himself | herself |
| itself | ourselves | yourselves | themselves |

EXAMPLES:

She prepared **herself** for the interview.

Carl blamed **himself**.

The reflexive pronoun refers to (or reflects back to) the subject of the sentence. It must be the appropriate pronoun to use with the subject.

pronoun	reflexive pronoun
I	myself
you (singular)	yourself
he	himself
she	herself
it	itself
we	ourselves
you (plural)	yourselves
they	themselves

Relative pronouns

who   whom   whose   which   that

For joining sentences

Relative pronouns are used to refer to the nouns or pronouns which have already been used earlier in a sentence. They are very useful for joining two sentences together.

e.g. There is the girl. Her mother designs clothes for 'Coronation Street'.

There is the girl whose mother designs clothes for 'Coronation Street'.

'whose' refers to the noun 'girl' and is used to join two simple sentences together.

e.g. He is the man. He rescued my kitten.

He is the man who rescued my kitten.

'who' refers to the noun 'man'.

13

- **who, whom** are used for people.
- **whose** is generally used for people but can refer to things.
- **which** is used for things and animals.
- **that** is a relative pronoun when it is used to replace 'which'. It is used for things and people.

Using relative pronouns

** Put the correct relative pronoun in each space:

1 I play squash with Diane .... lives next door to me.

2 This is the book .... I have been trying to buy.

3 The elephant is the animal .... I most admire.

4 He made notes about the picture .... had been stolen.

5 He hurried to help the boy .... foot was caught in the wire.

Whom

This is the object form of 'who' and is used in a clause to refer to the object of a verb.

e.g. Bill recognised the girl whom he had met at the dance.

This sentence is formed from the two sentences:

Bill recognised the girl. He had met her at the dance.

'her' is the object of the verb 'met', so when a relative pronoun is used to replace 'her' the object form 'whom' is chosen.

In speech, you would perhaps say, and might also hear others say: "Bill recognised the girl who he had met at the dance."

Although 'whom' is the correct form for writing, 'who' is widely used and accepted in speech.

'whom' is used after a preposition.

EXAMPLES:

The girl **to** whom he was talking was Hazel's sister.

The man **with** whom I was travelling had just completed his first novel.

Leaving out the relative pronoun

Often we omit the relative pronoun.

EXAMPLES:

Wear the tie that I gave you.✔

Wear the tie I gave you.✔

I have a copy of the book which you need.✔

I have a copy of the book you need.✔

Other functions

who, whom, whose, which, that do **not** always perform the function of relative pronouns. Look at the following sections about interrogative and demonstrative pronouns. (See also Chapter 15.)

Interrogative pronouns

The pronouns **who, what, whose, whom** and **which** are used to ask questions.

EXAMPLES:

Who wants another helping?

What is in the suitcase?

Whose is that?

Whom is it by?

Which is correct?

You will now see that 'who', 'what', 'whose', 'whom', 'which' can be relative or interrogative pronouns according to the way they are used in sentences.

EXAMPLES:

Which station is more convenient?

What action will you take?

Whose coat is that?

In these sentences 'which', 'what', 'whose' are not pronouns as they do not replace nouns. They go with the noun that follows them and so are considered to be adjectives. There is more about them in Chapter 15.

Demonstrative pronouns

singular	plural
this	these
that	those

EXAMPLES:

Lindsey gave this to me.   That is mine.

These are my heroes.   I hate those.

These words replace nouns and point out or demonstrate a particular thing or person.

The words 'this', 'that', 'these', 'those' can have other uses in sentences.

EXAMPLES:

This room is disgusting.   That tree is dangerous.

These cakes are delicious.   Those men are hungry.

In these sentences 'this', 'that', 'these', 'those' are each used with a noun so they are considered to be adjectives.

Other pronouns

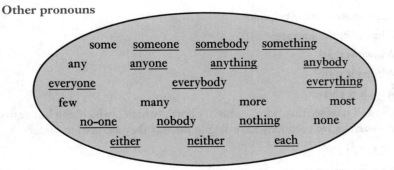

All of these words can be pronouns when they are used to replace a noun.

EXAMPLES:

Nobody is allowed in here.

Everyone is worried.

In the circle above, all the pronouns that are underlined need a singular verb when they are used as the subject of a sentence (see the examples above).

All the pronouns which need a singular verb need singular personal pronouns.

e.g. Nobody can do his best all the time.

In speech we often use a plural pronoun.

e.g. Everyone completed their work.

But in writing we should remember to use a singular pronoun.

either, neither, each, some, any, few, many, more can all be adjectives according to the way they are used in sentences.

e.g. **Each** person was given £5.

It is important to understand the work that pronouns do so that you can choose the exact pronoun for a given situation. Using pronouns correctly helps you to write clear and precise English.

More pronoun practice

** Find a suitable pronoun to use in each of these sentences.

1 .... is a temporary situation.

2 .... is marketing .... as the best political party for the '90s.

3 .... is preferable?

4 .... are outdated.

5 The boy .... won the competition is over there.

6 My boss and .... will arrive at 7 pm.

7 I suppose I must do it ....

8 .... are you doing?

1

14
Verbs

Although you will probably be aware of verbs, you may not be familiar with some of the terms that are used in this chapter. Don't worry. There is no need to learn the terms; the important thing is to understand how verbs work and to use them correctly in sentences.

What is a verb?

EXAMPLES:

Lucy was eating a sandwich.

The cat played with a mouse.

The builders worked until 6.00 pm.

He writes very neatly.

In each of these sentences an action is taking place. The actions are indicated by the words in colour.

A word which expresses an action is a verb. A verb can also indicate a state of being.

EXAMPLES:

She is fourteen.

I am a woman.

Verbs in sentences

As you saw in Chapter 2, a sentence is made up of two parts: the subject (who or what the sentence is about) and the predicate (which tells us more about the subject). A verb is the most important part of the predicate. A predicate must contain a verb.

subject	predicate	verb
Jonathan	sold his motorbike.	sold
I	like chocolate biscuits.	like
Easter	is in March this year.	is
The computer	developed a fault.	developed

You may have noticed that in these examples the verb consists of one word. Sometimes a verb needs two or three words to complete it.

EXAMPLES:

I am going to Birmingham.

   verb

Sheila had spoken

      verb

Lorraine will be telephoning later.

            verb

Auxiliary verbs

In the previous examples 'am', 'had' and 'will be' were required to help form the tense of the main verbs and so indicate *when* the actions occurred; 'am, 'had' and 'will be' are the auxiliary verbs in these sentences. Auxiliary verbs support the main verb in a sentence. They can be used to indicate tense and help form questions. The most common auxiliary verbs are formed from the verbs **to be, to have** and **to do.**

EXAMPLES:

Do you like coffee?

auxiliary verb main verb

He is visiting his sister.

auxiliary verb main verb

Have you finished your meal?

auxiliary verb main verb

Although the verbs formed from 'to be', 'to have' and 'to do' may be used as auxiliary verbs, they can also be used as the main verbs in sentences.

EXAMPLES:

Chris is 40 today.

main verb from 'to be'

Reg has three children.

main verb from 'to have'

I do the crossword puzzle every Sunday.

main verb from 'to do'

Other auxiliary verbs include:

can (I can swim.)

should (He should arrive shortly.)

may (May I come in?)

must (Sally must ask me.)

would (He would drive on Sunday.)

Formation of verbs

When forming verbs, you must beware of:

▶ agreement

▶ tense

Agreement

A verb has to agree with its subject.

Verb forms can differ according to whom is carrying out the action. The correct form of the verb must be chosen for that person. For example, look at the way the verb 'to walk' is formed in the present simple tense.

	singular	plural
first person	I walk	we walk
second person	you walk	you walk
third person	he/she/it walks	they walk

Helpful Hints

's' is added to the verb in the third person singular – this pattern is common to most other verbs in the present tense.

EXAMPLES:

she thinks   he swims   it falls

136

The verb 'to be' is irregular and has more changes of form.

present simple tense	past simple tense
I am	I was
you are	you were
he/she/it is	he/she/it was
we are	we were
they are	they were

As you can see, if you were to say:

I walks. ✗

you would be using the wrong form of the verb for the subject. The subject and verb would not agree.

Similarly, if you wrote:

They is walking up the street. ✗

you would also be incorrect. The correct form of the auxiliary verb to use in this sentence is 'are' (third person plural).

They are walking up the street. ✓

If English is your first language, you may choose the right form of the verb because you assimilated the correct constructions while you were learning to speak. However, if you are learning a foreign language it may take a considerable amount of practice to make the correct choice every time.

Practising correct agreement

** Choose the correct verb form in the following sentences.

1 He has/have finished the decorating.

2 There is/are twenty people waiting.

3 The shop is/are having an autumn sale.

4 Kate usually write/writes to me.

5 The office are/is closed all day.

Double subjects

Where the subject of a sentence is made up of two or more separate subjects, the verb is generally used in the plural form.

EXAMPLES:

Mr and Mrs Brewster are coming to dinner.

third person plural

The <u>manager</u> and her <u>assistant</u> were at the meeting.

third person plural

The <u>weather</u>, the drab <u>surroundings</u> and the poor <u>facilities</u> were all responsible for our miserable holiday.

third person plural

Singular words

In Chapter 12 you saw that a few common nouns appear to be plural but are used with a singular verb form.

EXAMPLES:

Rickets is almost unknown in this country today.

Mathematics is my worst subject.

Here are some other words which may cause confusion.

anybody	everybody	nobody
anyone	everyone	either
each	everything	neither

These words are used with a singular verb.

EXAMPLES:

Everything has been checked.

Neither of them is allowed in.

Helpful Hints

Confusion can arise when the word placed immediately before the verb appears to indicate a plural subject. Compare these sentences.

The competitors **have** to sign on. (The implied subject is 'all the competitors' so a plural verb is used.)

Each of the competitors **has** to sign on. (The implied subject is 'each individual competitor' so a singular verb is required.)

The trolley of groceries **was** left outside the shop. (The subject is one trolley of groceries so a singular verb is needed).

If you are in doubt, consider the subject of the sentence carefully and follow the guideline:

> a single subject requires the singular form of a verb;
>
> a plural subject requires the plural form of a verb.

Collective nouns

As you saw in Chapter 12, collective nouns (naming a complete set or group) are generally considered as a single unit and so take the singular verb form.

EXAMPLES:

The Conservative party is going to fight the next election.

The herd thunders across the plain.

but

My family have very different views on the subject.

In the last sentence, it is understood that the family is made up of a number of separate members each having different views, not a single unit, so a plural verb is used.

If the collective noun is a **single unit**, use a **singular verb form**. If the **separate parts** of the unit are being stressed, use a **plural verb form**.

More agreement practice

** Choose the correct form of the verb in each of these sentences.

1 The whole family is/are coming to dinner.

2 Only one of the children has/have survived.

3 The car and the lorry was/were involved in the crash.

4 Everyone in the room is/are busy.

5 The library has/have twenty thousand books.

6 Either he leave/leaves or I do.

7 Neither of the two boys was/were guilty.

8 A house and a bungalow in my street has/have been burnt down.

9 The bunch of flowers you sent has/have just arrived.

10 The news of his capture is/are very surprising.

Section 2

14

Tense

Look at these sentences:

Sentence 1 It is snowing.

Sentence 2 Chester bought a new table.

Sentence 3 Sue will be working here.

Although words like 'yesterday', 'now' or 'tomorrow' haven't been used, we understand that:

Sentence 1 is happening now (present)

Sentence 2 has already happened (past)

Sentence 3 will happen (future)

A verb in a sentence shows the time when an action takes place.

The form can show:

   present tense

   past tense

   future tense

Most verbs follow a pattern in forming each of these tenses and are referred to as regular verbs.

Present tense

This can be shown in two ways.

e.g. I eat. (present simple tense)

   I am eating. (present continuous tense)

Most verbs add an 's' for the third person singular in the present simple tense.

EXAMPLES:

She writes.

He sings.

Past tense

This can be shown in various ways.

EXAMPLES:

She watched the television. (past simple tense)

I was talking to Rob. (past continuous tense)

He has mended the window. (present perfect tense)

He had drunk half the bottle of whisky. (pluperfect tense)

In the past simple tense most regular verbs end in 'ed'

e.g. I **cooked** the dinner.

but a few verbs can end in either 't' or 'ed'.

EXAMPLES:

spoiled/spoilt

spelled/spelt

burned/burnt

kneeled/knelt

spilled/spilt

leaped/leapt

dreamed/dreamt

Irregular verbs form the past simple tense in a variety of ways.

EXAMPLES:

Kathleen **drove** to Edinburgh.

Ali **spoke** about his life.

We **ran** to the bus stop.

Future tense

There are a number of ways of expressing future time in sentences but in general we use 'shall' or 'will' as the auxiliary verb, together with a main verb

EXAMPLES:

I **shall see** you later.

The factory **will close** on Friday.

Another way of expressing an intention to carry out an action in the future is to use the 'going to' construction.

e.g. We are **going to look** for some new curtains.

This construction should only be used in speech or in informal writing.

Guidance

Be aware of tense when writing. You may need to change tense several times in a piece of writing in order to show the various times when actions or events happen. **But don't just drift from one tense to another.**

e.g. I opened the door and he jumps out at me. ✗

    I open the door and he jumps out at me. ✓ (present)

    I opened the door and he jumped out at me. ✓ (past)

14

The past tense is generally used to recount events. Occasionally a writer may use the present tense for effect but this can be difficult to sustain.

Don't worry about the various names of the tense forms. The names aren't important but knowing the various ways to use tenses in English may help you when you are learning foreign languages. If English is your second language, it is very useful to be aware of the tense forms.

Active and passive verbs

What is the difference between these two sentences?

Sentence 1 Peter Shilton kicked the ball away from the goal area.

Sentence 2 The ball was kicked away from the goal area by Peter Shilton.

Both sentences convey the same information but in sentence 1, Peter Shilton (the subject) carried out the action. He kicked the ball. In sentence 2, the ball (the subject) had the action done to it. It was kicked.

When the subject of a clause carries out the action, the verb is said to be 'active' but if the subject has the action done to it, the verb is said to be 'passive'.

Normally we use active verbs in our writing as they help to create a more direct and less wordy style.

Common confusions

was/were

As you have seen in this chapter, the usual pattern of the verb 'to be' in the past simple tense is

I was

you were

he/she/it was

we were

they were

but in certain cases 'were' is used for the 'I' and 'he'/'she'/'it' constructions.

After 'if'

EXAMPLES:

If I were a rich man, I'd ... .

If I were you, I would keep quiet.

EXAMPLES:

Tom behaves as if he were the manager.

The dog acted as though it were hungry.

Ambiguity

What is wrong with this sentence?

Running down the road, the car hit him.✗

The sentence does not instantly make sense. Because of the way it has been constructed, the phrase beginning with the present participle, 'running', relates to the word 'car' not to 'him'. A clearer way of expressing the idea is

Running down the road, he was hit by a car.✔

or

He was hit by a car while he was running down the road.✔

While it is possible to start a sentence with a present participle, it must be placed close to the person or thing it relates to.

e.g. Climbing the mountain, he fell and injured himself.✔

Final thoughts

Verbs play a crucial part in sentence construction. Most of the time we use them correctly without having to consider why we have made the choice or how we are using them. An understanding of the functions verbs perform in sentences can help us to write more accurately and avoid common mistakes.

This chapter contains a considerable amount of information about verbs. If you have found it difficult to assimilate all the ideas from one reading, it may be necessary to refer to certain sections again.

Section 2

14

15
Adjectives

What is an adjective?

EXAMPLES:

An unusual <u>smell</u> wafted from the narrow <u>doorway</u>.

The thin <u>boy</u> held a torn, yellow <u>flag</u> in his right <u>hand</u>.

The words in coloured type are all adjectives. Each adjective tells us more about a noun. The nouns they describe are underlined.

Adjectives usually go before the noun they describe but they can be placed elsewhere in the sentence.

EXAMPLES:

This <u>tomato</u> is soft and mouldy.

My <u>suitcase</u> is heavy.

In these two sentences the adjectives appear after the nouns they describe. As you will have noticed, a noun can be described by more than one adjective.

e.g. Four, trembling, tortoise-shell <u>kittens</u> were asleep in the basket.

An adjective gives us more information about a noun and can be placed before or after the noun it describes.

Adjectives improve writing

Choose adjectives carefully. If you painted a picture, you would try to use the exact shades of colour to make your painting accurate and realistic. The same idea applies to the choice of adjectives in writing – they are your 'shades of colour'.

Sometimes it is a good idea to use several adjectives which are similar in meaning in order to create atmosphere or clarity, but don't overdo this by using long lists of adjectives; the quality is more important than the quantity.

A dictionary and thesaurus will help you to choose and use the correct adjectives.

Some adjectives (such as 'big', 'nice' and 'lovely') are used so frequently that they become almost meaningless.

They give only a vague picture and should be replaced where possible by more precise adjectives. (In the vocabulary book in this *Getting to Grips* series, more advice is given about choosing adjectives.)

A   B

JANUARY MONDAY

On Sunday we went on an outing to Ironbridge. There are several museums and we decided to visit Blists Hill Museum. This museum allows visitors to see what life was like in late Victorian England.

We walked along the streets and looked around the shops. In each shop a shopkeeper talked about his life. Each was dressed in authentic costume.

My favourite shop was the chemist's with its four glass jars, each filled with water - the traditional symbols of a chemist's shop. The wooden fittings were original and were crammed with toiletries, packets, herbs and spices.

JANUARY MONDAY

On Sunday we went on an interesting day's outing to Ironbridge. There are several industrial museums and we decided to visit the fifty-acre Blists Hill Museum. This spectacular, open-air museum allows visitors to see what everyday life was like in late Victorian England.

We walked along the gaslit streets and looked around the small crowded shops. In each shop a knowledgeable and friendly shopkeeper talked about his working life. Each was dressed in authentic costume, newly laundered and neatly starched.

My favourite shop was the chemist's with its four large glass jars, each filled with coloured water - yellow, blue, green and red - the traditional symbols of a chemist's shop. The polished wooden fittings were original and were crammed with sweet-smelling toiletries, fading packets, and aromatic herbs and spices.

Which piece of writing gives you the clearer picture? Both passages are about the same subject, but by using additional adjectives passage B paints a more vivid picture and gives more details. The additional details make the passage more interesting and informative.

15

Proper adjectives

Some adjectives require capital letters. These are called proper adjectives as they are formed from proper nouns. You read about these in Chapter 4.

EXAMPLES:

The French language is very musical.

A Russian trawler docked in Aberdeen.

Lent is part of the Christian tradition.

There are many Islamic sects.

My uncle is Swedish.

Possessive adjectives

my, your, his, her, its, our and **their** can all be possessive adjectives as they indicate who the owner is.

EXAMPLES:

my hockey stick

your uncle

his memory

her behaviour

its mechanical parts

our patio

their family

'his', 'her', 'its' are also mentioned in Chapter 13. When you want to work out whether these three words are pronouns or adjectives, think about their functions.

An **adjective** provides more information about a noun.

e.g. Shahim placed her hand on its muzzle.

        adjective noun **adjective** noun

A pronoun replaces a noun.

e.g. Phil cannot hear her.

        object form of personal pronoun

Demonstrative adjectives

this, that, these and **those** are all demonstrative adjectives when they are linked with a noun.

EXAMPLES:

This duster is filthy.

That vase is beautiful.

These biscuits are burnt.

I enjoyed those poems.

As you saw in Chapter 13, when the same words are used to replace nouns, they are demonstrative pronouns.

e.g. I ordered that.

demonstrative pronoun

Interrogative adjectives

which, **what** and **whose** can all be used as questioning or interrogative adjectives when they accompany a noun. You may like to look back at interrogative and relative pronouns so that you make certain that you understand the other functions of these words.

EXAMPLES:

Which department is the largest?

What compensation can he expect?

Whose easel is this?

Adjectives of quantity

Some words can be used as adjectives to indicate quantity.

EXAMPLES:

five diaries	much food	little money
eighty sheep	many airmen	more mistakes
sixth position	several people	some words
	most accidents	few members

These adjectives give an exact quantity.

These adjectives do not indicate a precise amount.

Other adjectives

every, **each**, **either** and **neither** can all be adjectives when they are used to describe nouns.

15

EXAMPLES:

Either product is suitable.

Neither candidate impressed the interviewer.

The governors studied each possibility.

Every book on the subject has been borrowed.

▶ every, each, either, neither are followed by a singular verb.

▶ either and or go together.
e.g. I'd like to visit either Spain or Portugal.

▶ neither and nor go together.
e.g. Neither Joseph nor Danny was interviewed.

▶ When two different plural classes of people or things are referred to, a plural verb is needed.

EXAMPLES:

Neither earrings nor necklaces are allowed in this school.

Either councillors or officers are to blame.

Pronouns or adjectives?

As you will have seen, certain words can be pronouns or adjectives according to their function in a sentence.

** Classify as pronoun or adjective the underlined words in each sentence.

1 Which scarf is yours?

2 What work does he do?

3 This curry is more spicy than his.

4 He thinks that office needs redecorating.

5 Every idea is considered.

6 I would always choose these in preference to those.

7 I received those leaflets from him this morning.

8 Our house is old and ramshackle.

Using adjectives for comparison

DAVID   I prefer the Plymouth to Roscoff crossing.

ALISTAIR   Portsmouth to Le Havre is the shorter route.

KEVIN   We always travel on the shortest route – Dover to Calais.

DAVID   Is that the cheapest route too?

KEVIN   I don't know. My wife always insists on the short route.

In this conversation, adjectives are being used for comparison.

'the short route' This is called the **positive** form of the adjective. We are using it in a very positive or precise way. No comparison is taking place.

'the shorter route' This is the **comparative** form. It is used when we want to compare two items with one another.

'the shortest crossing' This is the **superlative** form. It should be used to compare three or more items.

Single-syllable adjectives

'short' is a one syllable word.

'shorter' – 'er' is added in the comparative form.

'shortest' – 'est' is added in the superlative form.

When you want to use the comparative or superlative forms of an adjective that consists of a single syllable, add er/est.

positive	comparative	superlative
bright	brighter	brightest
sweet	sweeter	sweetest
tall	taller	tallest
high	higher	highest

Two or more syllables

When an adjective has two or more syllables, we usually put the words more/most in front of the adjective to make the comparative/superlative forms.

e.g. Paris is a more attractive city than London.

'at/trac/tive' has three syllables so 'more' is used for the comparative and 'most' for the superlative.

Paris is the most attractive city in Europe.

Section 2

15

149

EXAMPLES:

positive	syllables	comparative	superlative
cautious	2	more cautious	most cautious
anxious	2	more anxious	most anxious
dramatic	3	more dramatic	most dramatic
amusing	3	more amusing	most amusing
comfortable	4	more comfortable	most comfortable
intelligent	4	more intelligent	most intelligent

but

positive	syllables	comparative	superlative
lucky	2	luckier	luckiest
pretty	2	prettier	prettiest
happy	2	happier	happiest

The last three examples seem to disobey the guidelines. Words such as these, ending in 'y' which makes a long 'e' vowel sound, usually take er/est for their comparative/superlative.

Changes to spelling

You will have noticed that with an adjective ending in 'y', the 'y' changes to 'i' before the endings er/est.

This rule applies to one-syllable words as well.
e.g. dry (drier, driest)

It applies to all adjectives ending in 'y' when there is a consonant before the final 'y'.

(If you want more information about such spelling changes, use the spelling book in this *Getting to Grips* series.)

positive	comparative	superlative
fat	fatter	fattest
slim	slimmer	slimmest
hot	hotter	hottest
thin	thinner	thinnest

Such single-syllable words double their final consonants before the endings er/est. Follow the guideline:

Is the adjective a one-syllable word?   YES

Is there one consonant at the end?   YES

Is there one vowel before this final consonant? YES

Then double the last letter.

Irregular words

There are certain common adjectives which do not obey the guidelines. Their comparatives and superlatives are totally irregular.

positive	comparative	superlative
good ——→	better	best
bad ——→	worse	worst
much ——→	more	most
many ——→	more	most
little ——→	less	least

EXAMPLES:

I have good eyesight.

Alex has better eyesight.

Clara has the best eyesight.

Adjectives without comparatives/superlatives

Some adjectives have no comparative or superlative forms.
e.g. 'round', 'square' and 'rectangular'

(An object cannot be 'rounder' than 'round'.)

e.g. 'right' and 'wrong'

These are precise terms and no comparison can be used.

e.g. 'unique'

As this word means there is only one of its kind, there can be no comparisons such as 'more unique' or 'most unique'. People often use 'unique' to mean 'unusual' but this is incorrect.

Using the guidelines

** Complete each space by choosing the correct comparative or superlative form of the adjective given in brackets:

Although Steve is the .... (young) in his class, he is the .... (good)

runner. Last year he was the .... (fast) sprinter in his year.

His .... (old) brother, Alan, is good at sport too and ....

(enthusiastic) than his brother. He has entered .... (many) races than

Steve and is a .... (confident) athlete than his .... (young) brother. Sport is .... (important) for Alan than his studies. He is much .... (bad) than Steve at English and maths and probably the .... (bad) mathematician the school has ever known. Alan's .... (happy) moments are on the race track and he dreams of being St. Mark's .... (fine) sportsman.

Final thoughts

▶ Be aware of the effect that carefully chosen adjectives can have on your writing.

▶ Read well-written descriptive passages, noticing the range of adjectives used.

▶ If you want help with distinguishing adjectives from pronouns or adverbs, refer to Chapters 13 and 16 respectively.

16
Adverbs

What is an adverb?

The usual function of an adverb is to give more information about a verb.

EXAMPLES:

The cat <u>stretched</u> sleepily.

    <u>verb</u>   **adverb**

               tells us how the cat stretched

The parcel <u>arrived</u> yesterday.

     <u>verb</u>   **adverb**

               tells us when the parcel arrived

An adverb can also give more information about an adjective.

EXAMPLES:

He was very <u>tall</u>.

adverb <u>adjective</u>

tells us more about his 'tallness'

The weather was too <u>cold</u>.

           adverb <u>adjective</u>

tells us more about the 'coldness'

An adverb can also give more information about another adverb.

e.g. The dinner was cooked quite quickly.

                adverb   **adverb**

                modifies   tells us how

                'quickly'   it was cooked

The function of an adverb is to give more information about:

- a verb
- an adjective
- another adverb

The adverb is said to 'modify' that word.

Adverbs in sentences

As you can see from the previous examples, the adverb is usually placed near the verb, adjective or adverb it modifies. However, there are no precise guidelines to indicate where an adverb may be placed in a sentence – this depends on the type of adverb and the stress placed upon it. We usually rely upon our knowledge of grammar and an awareness of what sounds right.

EXAMPLES:

Slowly he crawled towards the door.

He crawled slowly towards the door.

He crawled towards the door slowly

In this instance it is acceptable to place the adverb in any of these positions.

Many adverbs end in 'ly'.

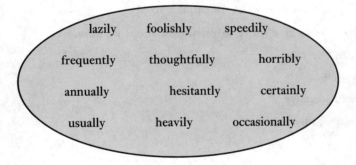

lazily　foolishly　speedily

frequently　thoughtfully　horribly

annually　hesitantly　certainly

usually　heavily　occasionally

When the 'ly' ending is added to a base word, the spelling can change.

EXAMPLES:

lazy + ly becomes **lazily** ('y' changes to 'i').

horrible + ly becomes **horribly** ('e' is dropped).

The spelling book in the *Getting to Grips* series gives more help with these spelling patterns.

Adverbs which do not end in 'ly' include:

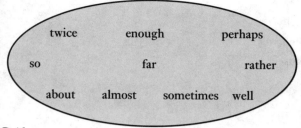

Guidance

A word may function as several different parts of speech. Look at how the word is being used in a sentence to decide which part of speech it is.

EXAMPLES:

He drove the <u>fast</u> car with skill and determination.

<u>adjective</u> describing the noun 'car'

He walked fast.

adverb modifying the verb 'walked'

How are adverbs used?

▶ Adverbs of manner
▶ Adverbs of time
▶ Adverbs of place
▶ Adverbs of degree
▶ Sentence adverbs

Adverbs of manner

EXAMPLES:

She spoke eagerly

She spoke reluctantly

She spoke hesitantly

The adverbs in these sentences provide information about <u>how</u> the actions are carried out. They are adverbs of manner. They are often formed from the corresponding adjective and frequently end in 'ly'.

16

EXAMPLES:

adjective	adverb
frugal	frugally
contented	contentedly
profuse	profusely

Adverbs of time

EXAMPLES:

The paint will be dry soon

The paint will be dry tomorrow

The paint will be dry eventually.

These adverbs tell us <u>when</u> the actions are carried out. They are adverbs of time and indicate not only when an action occurs but also how often.

e.g. He visits the park **daily**.

and for how long it continues.

e.g. He visited Paris **briefly**.

Adverbs of place

EXAMPLES:

Come here.

Come in.

Come away.

These adverbs tell the reader <u>where</u> the actions are carried out. They are adverbs of place and are usually placed next to the verb they modify. They do not end in 'ly'.

Adverbs of degree

These can be used to modify verbs, adjectives and other adverbs. They <u>give emphasis to or 'limit'</u> the word they modify.

EXAMPLES:

This is so difficult.

This is extremely difficult.

This is fairly difficult.

Interrogative adverbs

In previous chapters you have read about interrogative pronouns (who, what, whose, whom, which) and interrogative adjectives (what, whose, which). The other question words, **how, where, when, why** are interrogative adverbs and ask about the <u>manner</u>, <u>place</u>, <u>time</u> or <u>reason for</u> actions.

EXAMPLES:

How did you fall?

When did you fall?

Where did you fall?

Why did you fall?

Helpful Hints

where, when and **why** are not always used to ask questions.

EXAMPLES:

That is the house **where** the fire occurred.

I'm not sure **why** he is unhappy.

They will be here **when** they are ready.

In these sentences 'where', 'when' and 'why' are used to link two parts of a sentence.

Sentence adverbs (asides)

These are used to <u>express an opinion</u> and are often placed at the beginning of sentences.

EXAMPLES:

Perhaps he will decide to stay.

Unfortunately, she is ill.

Certainly, I'll check it for you.

Adverbs can improve writing

As you saw in Chapter 15, by using descriptive words in your writing you can create a more vivid and precise picture. Adverbs can also add colour and precision.

Compare these two sentences.

Tim spoke about his holiday in New Zealand.

Tim spoke enthusiastically about his holiday in New Zealand.

The addition of the adverb in the second sentence gives us a clearer idea of Tim's feelings about his holiday.

However if too many adverbs are used in a piece of writing, it can become tedious and contrived.

> "Where have you been?" Julian demanded angrily.
> "Nowhere," she replied defensively.
> He strode purposefully towards her. Louise edged timidly back until finally reaching the door, she ran swiftly from the room.
> Julian shouted apologetically after her, "Come back.. I forgive you."

Care should also be taken to choose appropriate adverbs for the situation.

** Select a variety of suitable adverbs for each of these verbs.

talked   fight   argued   think

sleep   played   cook   run

Using adverbs for comparison

EXAMPLES:

I worked hard on Saturday.

She worked harder on Saturday.

They worked hardest on Saturday.

Adverbs, like adjectives, can be used in comparisons and have similar rules for forming the comparative and superlative.

Guidance

The comparative form is used to compare two actions with one another.

The superlative form is used to compare three or more actions.

Single-syllable adverbs

EXAMPLES:

adverb	comparative	superlative
fast	faster	fastest
long	longer	longest
near	nearer	nearest

Add **er** or **est** to form the comparative or superlative forms of adverbs that consist of one syllable.

Two or more syllables

EXAMPLES:

adverb	comparative	superlative
carefully	more carefully	most carefully
simply	more simply	most simply
gracefully	more gracefully	most gracefully

More or **most** is usually placed in front of adverbs of two or more syllables when we make the comparative or superlative forms.

Irregular words

Certain adverbs do not follow the guidelines and have different ways of forming their comparatives and superlatives.

EXAMPLES:

(The adjectival form is shown in brackets.)

adverb	comparative	superlative
well (good)	better (better)	best (best)
badly (bad)	worse (worse)	worst (worst)
much (much)	more (more)	most (most)
little (little)	less (less)	least (least)

Helpful Hints

The comparative and superlative forms are the same for both adverbs and adjectives but errors occur when **good** and **well, bad** and **badly** are confused.

If you have problems with these, think about the functions of adverbs (they modify verbs, adjectives and other adverbs) and adjectives (which describe nouns). Decide which part of speech is required in the sentence.

EXAMPLES:

He swims well/good.

An adverb is needed in this sentence to tell us how 'He swims'.

He swims well.✔

16

James drives badly/bad.

An adverb is required
to tell us more about
the verb 'drives'.

James drives badly.✓

Final thoughts

▶ Choose suitable adverbs to enhance your writing and speech.

▶ There are no firm rules for positioning adverbs in sentences but they are usually placed near the word they modify.

▶ Although it is not vital to recall the names of the various types of adverbs, knowing that a word is functioning as an adverb in a sentence allows you to check that you are using it correctly.

CHAPTER

17
Prepositions

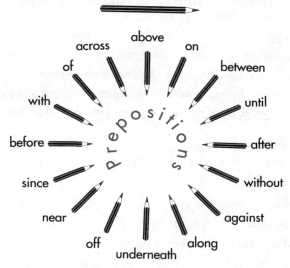

These are some of the words that can be used as prepositions. It is impossible to give a list of words that are *always* prepositions. Words can become different parts of speech according to how they are used in sentences. Some of the words above can also be used as adverbs. See the section **Preposition or adverb?** later in this chapter.

What is a preposition?

The word 'preposition' means 'place before'.

A preposition usually introduces a phrase containing a noun or pronoun.

EXAMPLES:

He waited for three <u>hours</u>.

      preposition   <u>noun</u>

Jenny reached towards <u>it</u>.

      preposition   <u>pronoun</u>

They decided to go on <u>Sunday</u>.

       preposition   noun

A preposition shows the relationship between the noun or pronoun it precedes and another word in the sentence. This relationship usually indicates time or place.

time	place
We will meet <u>at</u> four o'clock.	He rushed <u>through</u> the door.
I've been dieting <u>since</u> Christmas.	The cellar was <u>below</u> the stairs.
<u>After</u> his birthday, he went away.	The bus stop is <u>opposite</u> my house.
I left the pub <u>before</u> closing time.	He found the injured bird <u>under</u> a bush.

Complex prepositions

Sometimes two or three words are used together to function as a preposition.

EXAMPLES:

She walked away from the fire.

The paper is next to the typewriter.

Paul placed the card in front of the picture.

Preposition or adverb?

The difference between a preposition and an adverb can be summarised as follows: **A preposition shows a relationship; the main function of an adverb is to give more information about a verb.**

Some words can function as prepositions or adverbs.

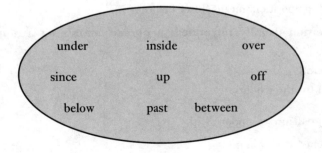

    under   inside   over

    since   up   off

    below   past   between

EXAMPLES:

The aeroplane flew over the house.

This is a **preposition** as it shows relationship.

David fell over.

This is an **adverb**; it gives more information about the verb.

He ran up the hill.

preposition

She looked up.

adverb

Using prepositions in sentences

EXAMPLES:

We drank coffee before the performance.

We drank coffee during the performance.

We drank coffee after the performance.

'before', 'during' and 'after' are prepositions which show the time relationship between the phrase 'drank coffee' and the noun 'performance'. By changing the preposition, we have altered the meaning of the sentences.

** Complete each of these sentences with a suitable preposition. Try to use as many different prepositions as possible.

1 Darren lives .... Brussels.

2 He leaned the ladder .... the wall.

3 The bus crashed .... a tree.

4 The book was taken .... the shelf.

5 Smoke .... the bonfire drifted .... the gardens.

6 Sarah complained .... her tutor .... the amount .... work she was expected to do.

Section 2

17

Correct choice

What is wrong with these sentences?

I insist about him doing it.✗

I'm bored of writing letters.✗

The inspector insisted they complied to his instructions.✗

In each sentence the wrong preposition has been chosen.

I insist on him doing it.✓

I'm bored with writing letters.✓

The inspector insisted they complied with his instructions.✓

Here are other examples of correct usage.

He was asked to refrain from smoking.

I was prevented from attending the meeting.

Paul was ashamed of his behaviour.

I was embarrassed by my mistake.

The board of directors approved of the new plan.

Unfortunately there isn't a set of guidelines to help us to select the correct preposition for each occasion. We learn correct usage by reading, listening and practising. If you are learning a foreign language, you may well encounter problems with prepositions. In most languages, selecting the appropriate preposition can be difficult. In English, one reason for this confusion is that a particular word can be followed by different prepositions according to its context.

EXAMPLES:

He acted on my advice.

Henry is acting with Sarah in the new play.

Hettie often acts against her husband's best interests.

More preposition practice

** Complete each of these sentences with the correct preposition:

1 My son was blamed .... the accident.

2 He is incapable .... making friends.

3 This is inferior .... the wine we bought last week.

4 I am conscious .... my appalling Spanish accent.

5 Sam approved .... his determination.

6 I would like to change this cardigan .... a larger size.

7 His uncle was compelled .... give up his job.

8 Rosita was prevented .... attending the concert.

As you will have noticed throughout this book, certain grammatical points change over a period of time – 'different from' is such an example. It is the correct combination for writing but 'different to' is becoming increasingly acceptable in speech.

Pronouns after prepositions

Which of these sentences is correct?

He gave it to I.

He gave it to me.

In Chapter 13, you saw that the object form of the personal pronoun is used when it follows a preposition. The object forms of personal pronouns are **me, you, him, her, it, us, them.**

He gave it to me. ✔

Where two different personal pronouns follow a preposition both are used in the object form.

e.g. He sent presents to **her** and **me**.

Selecting the correct pronouns

** Choose the correct pronouns to complete the sentences.

1 (She/Her) spoke to (me/I) about the new rosters.

2 The work was shared between (they/them) and (we/us).

3 The invitation was sent to my wife and (me/I).

4 They awarded one prize to (he/him) and another to (me/I).

5 According to (her/she), the prospects are encouraging.

Section 2

17

Over to You

The grammar of any language is the set of conventions which allows us to understand one another and helps us convey our message in a clear, precise and unambiguous way. It involves knowing about the work that words perform in a sentence.

You may not remember all the information that you have read in this grammar section; indeed, it is not intended that you should be able to recall all the technical terms. The important thing is to understand the function of words in sentences and use correct grammatical constructions.

Throughout this book we have tried to give advice about the avoidance of common errors. It is a good idea to go back over these notes from time to time to jog your memory.

As you check your writing you may have doubts about whether or not you are correct. Go back to the relevant chapter and check. By doing this you will gradually gain a firm understanding of all the grammar and punctuation points. Occasionally, you may only need to use the glossary in order to ensure that you are correct.

The more practice you give yourself in reading and writing, the more conversant you will become with grammar and punctuation. Familiarity will help you to develop more confidence in your style of writing and so you should gain more enjoyment from it.

Understanding the Terms

adjective, describes or gives more information about a noun.

    demonstrative adjective indicates a particular person or object.

    interrogative adjective accompanies a noun and introduces a question.

    possessive adjective describes a noun, indicating who the owner is.

    proper adjective is formed from a proper noun and requires a capital letter.

adverb, usually gives more information about a verb – explaining when, how or where an action takes place. It can also give additional information about an adjective or another adverb.

apostrophe, a raised comma (') which can show that a letter or letters have been omitted from a word **or** is used to indicate ownership.

brackets, a pair of brackets divides an additional fact, explanation, comment or afterthought from the rest of the sentence.

clause,

    main clause or independent clause makes complete sense and can stand alone as a sentence or make the main statement within a sentence.

    subordinate clause or dependent clause is part of a sentence. It does not make complete sense by itself but depends upon the main clause for sense.

colon, can be used to introduce a list, speech or a quotation. It is often used to divide one part of a sentence from another when the second half explains, expands or summarises the first half.

comma, is used within a sentence to separate one group of words from another so that the meaning of the sentence is clear.

comparisons of adjectives,

    positive form of adjectives is used when no comparison is being made.

    comparative form of adjectives is used when two people or items are being compared with one another.

    superlative form of adjectives is used to compare three or more people or items.

conjunction, a word which links two parts of a sentence together.

consonant, any letter of the alphabet which is not a vowel.

contraction, two words joined together and shortened to form one word. An apostrophe is used to show that a letter or letters have been omitted.

dash, indicates a dramatic pause, an interrupted conversation, or introduces an explanation.

a pair of dashes, separates asides, afterthoughts, opinions or non-essential information from the main thrust of the sentence.

exclamation, a sentence which is expressed in an emotional way. The sentence ends in an exclamation mark.

exclamation mark, used at the end of an exclamatory sentence, interjection, or some commands.

full stop, used to end a sentence. It is also used in some abbreviations.

hyphen, used to join two or more words to make a single word.

interjection, a word or words which express an emotion. Interjections are used in speech and in written dialogue. An exclamation mark is placed after an interjection.

inverted commas, see 'quotation marks'.

noun, a word used to name a person, place, animal or thing.

> abstract noun names a quality, feeling or idea – something which is intangible.

> collective noun names a complete set or group.

> common noun is the general name for a person, place, animal or thing.

> proper noun names a particular person, building, country or company, etc.

object, the person or thing that an action is carried out upon.

phrase, a group of words which on its own does not make complete sense.

predicate, contains a verb and provides information about the subject.

preposition, introduces a phrase containing a noun or pronoun and shows the relationship between this noun or pronoun and another word within the sentence. This relationship indicates time or place.

pronoun, a word used instead of a noun. It refers to a thing or person previously mentioned.

> demonstrative pronoun points out a particular thing or person.

> impersonal pronoun (one) refers to a person or people in a general way.

> interrogative pronoun replaces a noun and is used to ask a question.

personal pronoun changes its form according to whether it is the subject or object of a sentence.

possessive pronoun is used to show ownership. It does not require an apostrophe.

reflexive pronoun refers back to the subject of the sentence.

relative pronoun is used to refer to a noun or pronoun which has already been used earlier in the sentence. It can be used to join two sentences together.

question mark, used at the end of a sentence where an answer is expected.

quotation marks, can be double (" ") or single (' ') and are placed around the actual words a person says in dialogue, or around a quotation.

semicolon, links two closely related sentences into one longer sentence, or joins sentences which indicate a contrast. It can also be used to punctuate a long or complicated list.

sentence, a group of words which makes complete sense. It begins with a capital letter and ends with either a full stop, question mark or exclamation mark. A sentence must have a subject and a predicate.

simple sentence contains one verb and its subject.

double sentence is two simple sentences linked by a conjunction.

multiple sentence is more than two sentences linked by conjunctions.

complex sentence has at least one main clause and one or more dependent clauses.

speech,

direct speech consists of the actual words a person says in a dialogue. The words spoken are shown within quotation marks.

indirect speech conveys the content of the speech to the reader without quoting the actual words spoken.

subject, who or what a sentence is about.

verb, expresses an action or indicates a state of being.

auxiliary verb accompanies and helps a main verb.

vowel, there are five vowels in the English language: a, e, i, o, u.

Answers

N.B. No answers are given where you are asked to research words in a dictionary or thesaurus, where answers depend upon personal responses, or where a number of alternative answers is possible.

Chapter 2   Sentences

Punctuating sentences

1 Who is that person over there?
2 I hope he is all right.
3 What a lovely dog they have!
4 Don't do that. *or* Don't do that!
5 Please can I come with you?
6 I expect he'll be late tonight.
7 Follow the advice given on the packet.
8 Which restaurant shall we go to?

Identifying the subject and predicate

1 **Journalists** <u>were warned to stay clear of the area</u>.
    subject   predicate

2 **Fifteen thousand fans** <u>attended the concert</u>.
          subject   predicate

3 **Kurt** <u>plays squash regularly</u>.
  subject   predicate

4 **That young couple** <u>bought Norma's house</u>.
        subject   predicate

5 **The weather** <u>has been wonderful recently</u>.
      subject   predicate

6 **It** <u>must have cost a great deal</u>.
  subject   predicate

7 **Football** <u>is popular in many countries</u>.
      subject   predicate

8 **They** <u>were wrong</u>.
  subject   predicate

Finding the verb

1 ran
2 moved
3 sat
4 slept
5 invited
6 has
7 were
8 was

Finding the subject

1 He
2 The car
3 She
4 They
5 John and Sue
6 He
7 We
8 The book

Identifying sentences

1 Not a sentence
2 A sentence
3 Not a sentence
4 A sentence
5 A sentence
6 A sentence
7 A sentence
8 Not a sentence
9 A sentence
10 Not a sentence

Chapter 3   More about Sentences

Practising double sentences

1 The fire burnt down their house <u>but</u> most of their belongings were saved.

2 I hope to visit Moscow this summer <u>or/but</u> I could wait until next year.

3 The car stalled at the traffic lights <u>and</u> (it) could not be restarted.

4 Will you have some cake <u>or</u> would you prefer a biscuit?

5 Hal can swim half a mile <u>and</u> (he) can tread water for ten minutes.

6 The curry was soon ready <u>but</u> the basmati rice took longer to cook.

7 The brake pads appear to be worn <u>and</u> (they) need to be replaced.

8 Most Saturdays Peter plays football <u>but</u> sometimes he goes to watch rugby.

Chapter 4   Capital Letters

Using the guidelines

JOHN	Well, Officer, there were two blokes.
CLIFF	No, there were three. You forgot the driver in the light blue jumper who drove the green Landrover.
DAVE	Can I get a word in? The Landrover was dark blue and his jumper was turquoise.
POLICEMAN	Now, now, let's have some agreement. Just how many men were there? If we can all decide on that and the colour of the Landrover, it would be most helpful. Do any of you recall the registration number?

Capital letter practice

1 Nila had always wanted a Victorian brooch.

2 He has a Swiss passport.

3 In this country Asian culture is widely respected.

4 Holland has a great variety of excellent Indonesian restaurants.

5 Richard is very proud of his Mancunian accent.

6 The Russian army is used to harsh climatic conditions.

Practice

GALA DINNER IN AID OF MEDICAL RESEARCH

Guest List

President Bush   The Duke of Westminster
Queen Juliana   Lord Longford
Prince Harry   Captain Walker
Princess Caroline   Reverend Jackson
King Hussein   Professor Hoyle
Air Marshal Spencer Doctor Owen

Putting capital letters to the test

a Swiss national   London's Stock Exchange
the National Curriculum   the Indian cricket team
British Medical Association   the Great Barrier Reef
the Education Secretary   Arctic Ocean
Portuguese television   Shrove Tuesday
Toyota cars   President Gorbachev
Korean manufacturers   British Airways

1 He was a captain in the army.
2 The Empire State Building is a tourist attraction.
3 He wanted to train to be a doctor.
4 Clive is a government official in Swansea.
5 Every headmaster should receive some training in financial matters.
6 I always choose a country with mountains for my holiday.
7 Phil Bartlett has now become Bishop Bartlett.
8 Emma's special subject was the Romans.

---

9 My favourite book is 'The Wind in the Willows'.

10 Last year the whole family went to see the London Marathon.

You will have designed your own sentences but you will need capital letters for:

Chief Inspector Crump, New Zealander, Britain

I, Hull, Humberside

Jill Francis, Mr Oakham, Aunt Hilda, New Year's Day

Americans, French lessons, Spanish

Yours faithfully, Dear Sir

Wimbledon

Chapter 5   Punctuation in Practice

Sentence practice

> I went to see the film 'Heart Condition' last week. It stars Bob Hoskins who plays a racially intolerant New York policeman. After having a near fatal heart attack, he is given a heart transplant. He discovers that his new heart belonged to a black lawyer who returns to haunt him. It was a gripping film and one I would recommend.

Recognising questions

1 How is Beth after her accident?

2 Sid wanted to know if he could buy some books.

3 What is the time?

4 I wonder how much they charge.

5 Arif asked me to tell him about our holiday.

6 Where are Mr and Mrs Fisher?

7 Elaine asked why they were so late.

8 Alan wanted to know why he had been left out of the team.

Chapter 6   Introducing Commas

Commas in lists

The list within each sentence should be punctuated as follows:

Harveys and Taylor, Whittington and Craddock, Brewer and Turnbull, and Fletcher and Summers

mangoes, bananas, grapes, melons and plums

Mary Wesley, Agatha Christie and Leslie Thomas

Durham, Liverpool, Manchester, Preston, Bolton and Leeds
'The Rain Forest', and 'Kings and Queens of England'
Ovaltine and Horlicks

Test your comma skills

1 Family, friends, colleagues and business acquaintances were all invited to his fortieth birthday party.

2 She placed the cheque in the envelope, sealed the envelope, addressed it with care and checked it thoroughly before placing it next to the telephone.

3 The young child reached out for the soft, floppy, pink rabbit.

4 The group spent an enjoyable day visiting the Planetarium, feeding the ducks in St James's Park, watching the Changing of the Guard and shopping in Oxford Street.

5 Sieve the flour, cut up the fat into small cubes and weigh out the fruit.

6 Andrew requested, pleaded, demanded and threatened but his brother would not let him borrow the car.

7 He wrote slowly, deliberately and thoughtfully.

8 Her writing was large, untidy and illegible.

Chapter 7   More About Commas

Comma practice

Having spent the past week revising, he was confident about the examination. When the paper was placed on his desk, he felt excited and eager to begin.

As he turned over the page and noticed the first question, his heart began to pound. Despite all his revising, he would not be able to attempt question one. Resting his head in his hands, he tried to concentrate on the exact wording of the question, hoping he had misread it at his first attempt.

Using the guidelines

1 Our doctor, a member of the Territorials, was called up to serve in the Gulf War.

2 Our doctor, the most popular in the practice, is an army medical reserve.

3 Saumur, with its imposing chateau, is an excellent place to stay.

4 I found Norwegian, although similar to both Swedish and Danish, very difficult to learn.

5 Maureen, who used to live near us in Corby, has now moved to Northampton.

6 The sail-board, which we bought when we were on holiday, is too heavy for me.

7 As you know, I am not used to flying.

8 Tim, a previous county member, now plays for our team.

9 Clive, although very annoying at times, is usually good-tempered and reasonable.

10 The birthday card, made from recycled paper, was propped against the clock.

Commas for sense

1 According to Sue, Johnson is guilty.

2 You will not succeed however hard you work.

3 However, I don't wish to buy one.

4 After all, the girls knew.

5 In writing, a comma helps the reader.

6 He drove to the vet's with his girlfriend, and the hamster in the cage.

7 He carried the cat, and the flowers in water into the lounge.

Using commas

1 Two of them, including one aimed at the captain, were intercepted.

2 Our correspondent, Mark Lacey, saw it all happen.

3 After the school had been declared safe, the children returned to the classroom.

4 The soldier who went missing on the training mission was found unhurt.

5 Mr Kieron Stevenson, a 64-year-old married man, was appointed as the gardening club's new chairperson.

6 Lorries, many with foreign number plates, rumbled along the narrow road throughout the day, making the residents' lives miserable.

7 The headmaster, while sympathetic to the residents' complaints, said the school's new classrooms had to be built.

8 Having prepared himself well in advance, he felt relaxed.

9 "Would the lady to the right of the door please step forward."

10 That elderly man sitting on the green chair is next.

11 Yes, I know who you are talking about.

12 By the way, I will join you.

13 To walk under a ladder, so people say, is unlucky.

14 When I heard the news on the television last night, I was greatly distressed.

15 I was very upset when I heard the news.

16 The cat jumped on her lap, settled himself into a comfortable position and purred contentedly.

17 He dismissed, without a moment's hesitation, the idea of any employees being asked to move to the firm's branch in Blackpool.

Chapter 8   Apostrophes

Using apostrophes for contractions

don't	I'd
let's	haven't
who's	didn't
mustn't	hadn't
they'd	they're
doesn't	what's

Using apostrophes in dialogue

"It's two o'clock. We'll miss the train if we don't hurry," complained Mark.

"I can't find my keys. This drawer's full of rubbish. I'll never find them," wailed Jane.

"Let's leave them," Mark insisted. "We've only fifteen minutes left."

Jane shouted, "They're here, under the bureau! No wonder I couldn't see them."

Recognising the owner/s

1	plural	6	singular
2	singular	7	plural
3	plural	8	plural
4	singular	9	singular
5	singular	10	singular

	owner	owned		owner	owned
1	directors	secretaries	6	plant	roots
2	library	entire store	7	employees	files
3	candidates	papers	8	safes	contents
4	enemy	army	9	Mike	business
5	aeroplane	fuel tank	10	Adele	computer

Using apostrophes to show possession

1 the children's responsibility

2 its paintwork

3 men's interests

4 two girls' reputations

5 one's life

6 women's work

7 Yours was over there.

8 I know the ones you mean.

9 He was unaware that the car was theirs.

10 The sheep's wool was spun on the farm.

1 She hung up the ladies' clothes.

2 The double bass's case had been forced open.

3 The presses' guarantees had expired.

4 The class's teacher was new.

5 Peter Simms's/Simms' mother lives next door to me.

6 That is Miss Curtis's/Curtis' bicycle.

7 Mr Malpass's/Malpass' yacht won the race.

Using apostrophes to indicate time

1 a day's outing

2 in six months' time

3 four days' drive

4 five minutes' rest

5 three months' credit

6 a second's delay

7 a year's study

8 the season's programme

9 a good night's sleep

10 five weeks' marking

11 six years' work

12 a lifetime's wear

13 an afternoon's enjoyment

14 two years' secondment

15 a term's grant

16 two years' tax arrears

Putting apostrophes to the test

Suggestions:

1 St Mark's Church is in St James's/James' Street.

2 The outpatients' clinic is on the hospital's East Wing.

3 A week's holiday was followed by a term's work.

4 The man's suit hung next to the woman's cardigan.

5 The headmaster's study was full of the pupils' work.

6 The farmer's crops were damaged by the gale's ferocity.

1 a residents' association

2 the manageress's office

3 Pauline's umbrella

4 the window cleaner's ladder

5 my mother-in-law's friends

6 the Boys' Brigade

7 the pensioners' club

8 a robin's nest

9 the film's speed

10 the gardener's tools

MOTHER	I'd love to hear about him.
DAUGHTER	I can't think who you mean.
MOTHER	That new boyfriend of yours!
DAUGHTER	Isn't anything special to tell you.
MOTHER	What's his job?
DAUGHTER	He's twenty, unemployed, his name's Matthew, his mother's called Sally, his pets' names are Mrs P. and Mitten. Enough?
MOTHER	I've heard he lives in that large house next to the newsagent's.
DAUGHTER	So what?
MOTHER	His parents must be wealthy. Oh well, I suppose he won't be a bad lad if he comes from wealthy parents!

Chapter 9   Conversations and Quoting

Practising indirect speech

1 She explained that there had been an accident.

2 Mrs Roberts said that Neals are/were selling shoes at 50% off.

3 He said that his car seemed to have broken down.

4 Ian replied that he missed the train today/that day because his watch had stopped.

5 Mr Palmer said that it isn't/wasn't a good year for fruit.

6 She asked if she was/were expected to work in this/that mess.

7 Carol stated that she hasn't/hadn't had a puncture for years.

8 Barry said that he wasn't buying/wasn't going to buy/wouldn't be buying cheese from that shop again. The (as the) last lot was mouldy.

Using the guidelines

1 "I hope we will see you at the exhibition," said the salesman.

2 "Jane and Val work together in the same office," she said, "but they never speak to one another."

3 Mr Holdsworth said, "I shall have a good crop of potatoes this year."

4 "Last year we visited Scotland," Penny explained, "and we hope to visit it again this summer."

5 "My exam results were terrible," *or* "My exam results were terrible!" he confessed.

6 "The lounge and the dining room both need decorating," she said. "Have you any idea when you can do them?"

7 "Well," she said, "I am surprised!"

or "Well!" she said, "I am surprised."

8 "I see 'Brookside' is on at 7.00 pm tonight," Dorothy said. "I hope I'll be home in time."

9 "The sheep broke through a hole in the fence," he explained, "but we've managed to get them all back."

10 "Will you mend it for me," he asked, "or shall I return it to the shop?"

Chapter 10   Other Punctuation Points

Using semicolons

1 A Bactrian camel has two humps; a dromedary has a single hump.

2 Kerry hesitated as she went to slam the car door; she checked the keys were in her pocket.

3 I won't be home tonight; I have cricket practice.

4 Her operation had to be cancelled; this was a sensible decision as she had a cold.

5 The workforce walked out; they could not tolerate the situation any longer.

6 He won't be going to Switzerland for his holiday this year; he went there twice on business last month.

7 I am not going to the meeting tonight; I have a headache.

8 Barbara's first retail job was at Sainsbury's; her second was at Tesco's.

9 The golf ball hit the window; it broke the glass.

10 Each day I go to college by train; I could just as easily go by bus.

More semicolon practice

1 I have been sent to collect the following items: the Olivetti word processor with the built-in printer; the computer desk, delivered last week; a box of fifty discs, ordered from Rapid Foreward; two printer covers, discarded by the legal department(;) and a set of encyclopaedias.

2 Winter had arrived early that year: the drive had been a sheet of glistening ice for the past month; the ancient plumbing system, although its pipes had been wrapped in sacking, had completely frozen; each morning the insides of the windows were encrusted in ice(;) and for days they had been without electricity.

Using colons in lists

1 There-was a variety of vehicles in his drive: a caravan, a vintage car, a classic motorbike and a brand new Rolls Royce.

2 We visited four counties in all: Lancashire, Yorkshire, Durham and Northumberland.

3 She read three books during the Christmas holiday: 'The Naked Ape', '500 Mile Walkies' and 'Spycatcher'.

4 He applied to four universities: Cardiff, Kent, Leicester and Surrey.

5 "Which floor would you like: toys, furnishings or ladies' fashions?"

More colon practice

1 Shuffling the papers together, he came to a decision: he'd resign.

2 The birds scattered: they must have heard the cat.

3 The weather is the same every day: hot, dry and windy.

4 It was his most successful day so far: he had sold three cars.

5 Stella was bitterly disappointed: she had failed her driving test.

6 Bradley knew what he must do: marry her.

7 The young man had only one thought: revenge.

Using the single dash

1 I know now why I dislike Sue – she's dishonest.

2 History, geography, English, and religious education – these were his favourite subjects.

3 We cleared the snow from the shared drive – the neighbours stayed indoors.

4 I'll mend it for you – when I'm ready.

Using a pair of dashes

1 When Petronia returned home – it was later then usual – the suitcase was missing.

2 I saw that film – the last film to be shown there – at the Classic Theatre.

3 Last September – I was on holiday in France at the time – my car was broken into.

4 The whole school – pupils, staff, caretakers, ancillary workers – joined in the protest.

5 Your son's work – as I said at out last meeting – is careless and inadequate.

6 My car – a luxury model when it was new – now seems very uncomfortable and basic.

7 I understand your feelings – the same thing happened to me – but you must try to forget it.

8 As soon as he was promoted – he had applied for the post three times – he took the entire section to the pub.

9 Thousands of residents will be taking part in the National Census – set for April 21 – and the results will be used to plan development in the area.

10 I can understand your protesting – I would if I lived where you do – but I feel it will be quite futile.

Using brackets

1 to enclose dates

2 to show alternative measurements/conversions

3 distance in miles/kilometres

4 extra information

5 road number

6 page number

7 county distance

8 aside

Correct usage

1 Bradley plays on the right wing.

2 Our boss has left-wing tendencies.

3 The top-heavy basket fell over.

4 It was a hair-raising event.

5 Peter was a hard-working man

Chapter 12   Nouns

Identifying nouns

1 house, lake

2 company, fall, profits

3 typewriter

4 mountaineer

5 train, platform

6 watch

7 people, doors

8 tape, bag

9 mother, village

Recognising proper nouns

Jamaica, Big Ben, Manchester
Lent, Monday, Boxing Day, Eid, Friday
Derek, Dr Death, Fred
500 Owners' Association, Yorkshire Television, National Trust, Mercury
Communications, Midland Bank
Lassie, Fido
Marxism
Ford Escort

Proper nouns in context

Finland, Sweden, Norway and Denmark are four of Europe's
most northerly countries. Each is beautiful but none is
particularly popular with tourists from Britain. Part of
Finland lies to the north of the Arctic Circle where herds of
reindeer roam across the wilderness. The capital of Sweden is
Stockholm, an attractive city on the Baltic Sea. The person
most people associate with Denmark is the writer of fairy
stories: Hans Christian Andersen. Another name which will
be familiar to parents is Lego. Denmark is the home of Lego
and visitors can spend several happy hours walking around
Legoland.

Chapter 13   Pronouns

Using personal pronouns

1 He shared it between Liz and <u>him</u>.

2 Glenn begged, "Please come to stay with Helen and <u>me</u>."

3 The college was threatened with closure, but <u>it</u> has been given six months' reprieve.

4 "It's <u>she</u> you should ask," protested Tim.

5 <u>They</u> boycotted the meeting.

6 It is <u>they</u> who should be concerned about <u>him</u>.

Using relative pronouns

1 I play squash with Diane <u>who</u> lives next door to me.

2 This is the book <u>which/that</u> I have been trying to buy.

3 The elephant is the animal <u>which/that</u> I most admire.

4 He made notes about the picture <u>which/that</u> had been stolen.

5 He hurried to help the boy <u>whose</u> foot was caught in the wire.

More pronoun practice

1 <u>This/that/it</u> is a temporary situation.

2 <u>It</u> is marketing <u>itself</u> as the best political party for the '90s.

3 <u>Which/what/whose</u> is preferable?

4 <u>These/those/they</u> are outdated.

5 The boy <u>who</u> won the competition is over there.

6 My boss and <u>I/he/she</u> will arrive at 7 pm.

7 I suppose I must do it <u>myself</u>.

8 <u>What/which/whose</u> are you doing?

Chapter 14   Verbs

Practising correct agreement

1 He <u>has</u> finished the decorating.

2 There <u>are</u> twenty people waiting.

3 The shop <u>is</u> having an autumn sale.

4 Kate usually <u>writes</u> to me.

5 The office <u>is</u> closed all day.

More agreement practice

1 The whole family <u>is</u> coming to dinner.

2 Only one of the children <u>has</u> survived.

3 The car and the lorry <u>were</u> involved in the crash.

4 Everyone in the room <u>is</u> busy.

5 The library <u>has</u> twenty thousand books.

6 Either he <u>leaves</u> or I do.

7 Neither of the two boys <u>was</u> guilty.

8 A house and a bungalow in my street <u>have</u> been burnt down.

9 The bunch of flowers you sent <u>has</u> just arrived.

10 The news of his capture <u>is</u> very surprising.

Chapter 15   Adjectives

Pronouns or adjectives?

1 adjective, pronoun

2 adjective, pronoun

3 adjective, pronoun

4 pronoun, adjective

5 adjective

6 pronoun, pronoun, pronoun

7 pronoun, adjective, pronoun, adjective

8 adjective

Using the guidelines

Although Steve is the <u>youngest</u> in his class, he is the <u>best</u> runner. Last year he was the <u>fastest</u> sprinter in his year.

His <u>older</u> brother, Alan, is good at sport too and <u>more enthusiastic</u> than his brother. He has entered <u>more</u> races than Steve and is a <u>more confident</u> athlete than his <u>younger</u> brother. Sport is <u>more important</u> for Alan than his studies. He is much <u>worse</u> than Steve at English and maths and probably the <u>worst</u> mathematician the school has ever known. Alan's <u>happiest</u> moments are on the race track and he dreams of being St Mark's <u>finest</u> sportsman.

Chapter 17   Prepositions

Using prepositions in sentences

Suggested answers

1 Darren lives <u>in/near</u> Brussels.

2 He leaned the ladder <u>against</u> the wall.

3 The bus crashed <u>into</u> a tree.

4 The book was taken <u>off/from</u> the staff.

5 Smoke <u>from</u> the bonfire drifted <u>across/through</u> the gardens.

6 Sarah complained <u>to</u> her tutor <u>about</u> the amount <u>of</u> work she was expected to do.

More preposition practice

1 My son was blamed <u>for</u> the accident.

2 He is incapable <u>of</u> making friends.

3 This is inferior <u>to</u> the wine we bought last week.

4 I am conscious <u>of</u> my appalling Spanish accent.

5 Sam approved <u>of</u> his determination.

6 I would like to change this cardigan <u>for</u> a larger size.

7 His uncle was compelled <u>to</u> give up his job.

8 Rosita was prevented <u>from</u> attending the concert.

Selecting the correct pronouns

1 <u>She</u> spoke to <u>me</u> about the new rosters.

2 The work was shared between <u>them</u> and <u>us</u>.

3 The invitation was sent to my wife and <u>me</u>.

4 They awarded one prize to <u>him</u> and another to <u>me</u>.

5 According to <u>her</u>, the prospects are encouraging.

Index